VGM Opportunities Series

OPPORTUNITIES IN **RECREATION AND LEISURE CAREERS**

Clayne R. Jensen and Jay Naylor

Revised by
Holly Best

Foreword by
Roger L. Coles, Ed.D.
Department Chair, Recreation
Central Michigan University
and
Christen G. Smith, Ph.D.
Faculty
Aurora University (Illinois)

VGM Career Horizons
NTC/Contemporary Publishing Group

331.7
J S4

Library of Congress Cataloging-in-Publication Data
Jensen, Clayne R.
    Opportunities in recreation & leisure careers / Clayne R. Jensen
and Jay Naylor. — Rev. / by Holly Best.
        p.   cm. — (VGM opportunities series)
    Rev. ed. of: Opportunities in recreation and leisure careers.
©1990
    Includes bibliographical references (p.   ).
ISBN 0-8442-2985-7 (cloth). — ISBN 0-8442-3229-7 (pbk.)
        1. Recreation—Vocational guidance—United States.   2. Leisure—
Vocational guidance—United States.   I. Naylor, Jay H.
    II. Eberts, Marjorie.   III. Gisler, Margaret.   IV. Jensen, Clayne R.
Opportunities in recreation and leisure careers.   V. Title.
    VI. Title: Opportunities in recreation and leisure careers.
    VII. Series.
    GV160.J45   1999
    790'.023'73—dc21   99-34152
                                                                          CIP

Cover photographs: © PhotoDisc, Inc.

Published by VGM Career Horizons
A division of NTC/ Contemporary Publishing Group, Inc.
4255 West Touhy Avenue, Lincolnwood (Chicago), Illinois 60712-1975 U.S.A.
Printed in the United States of America
International Standard Book Number: 0-8442-2985-7 (cloth)
                                    0-8442-3229-7 (paper)
  99   00   01   02   03   04   LB   18   17   16   15   14   13   12   11   10   9   8   7   6   5   4   3   2   1

DEDICATION

This revised edition is dedicated to my family—the "Best" family a person could have. Without you I wouldn't be where I am today. You have pushed me to be the best that I can be and made me believe that all of my goals are attainable. Thank you for your unconditional love and endless support.

H.B.

CONTENTS

The total recreation experience. An important challenge.
Dealing with the misconceptions. Are you suited to the
challenge?

Divisions of recreation. Development of the recreation
profession.

Underlying forces of change.

Personal requirements. Professional goals.

Early career exploration. Status of professional preparation.
Professional preparation programs. Associate degree

programs. Bachelor degree programs. Graduate preparation. Scholarships and internships. Colleges and universities that offer curricula related to recreation and leisure.

ABOUT THE AUTHORS

After completing bachelor's and master's degrees and participating in athletic competition at the University of Utah, Clayne Jensen completed a three-year term of duty as a commissioned officer in the U.S. Marine Corps. After gaining additional professional experience, he joined the faculty and coaching staff at Utah State University. Among other teaching and coaching responsibilities, he worked as a recreation and park specialist for Utah's State Extension Service and was executive director of the State Interagency Council for Recreation.

Professor Jensen completed a doctorate degree at Indiana University in 1963 and has since occupied various teaching and administrative positions at Brigham Young University. He is currently dean of the College of Health, Physical Education, Recreation, and Athletics and has participated extensively in professional organizations, workshops, and conferences. Dr. Jensen has established himself as one of the most prolific authors in his field, having authored or co-authored sixteen textbooks, which are currently in print, as well as a large number of professional articles. Because of his achievements, he has received several athletic and professional service awards and has been listed in a number of biographical sources, including *Who's Who in America, Who's Who in Education, Who's Who in the West, International Bibliographies,* and *Men of Achievement.*

Clayne Jensen has remained an avid enthusiast of sports and outdoor recreation and is still both a student and a teacher of active and wholesome activities.

Jay Naylor received his B.S. and M.A. degrees in recreation management and physical education from Brigham Young University. He earned the Ed.D. degree from the University of Utah. His teaching experience has spanned more than twenty-six years at Brigham Young. He served for seven years as chairman of the Department of Recreation Management and Youth Leadership and is now the associate dean of the college. His professional experience includes work with the Los Angeles Parks and Recreation Department, Spokane Parks and Recreation (Washington), and as director of Pacific Palisades Youth Center in California. He has served as shipboard director of recreation for the Foreign Study League of Salt Lake City and as director of the Thames Valley Camp, Ponybourne, England, for the American Camps International. Later he served for two years as a member of the ACI Board of Directors.

This edition has been revised by Holly Best, who completed her B.S. degree in parks and recreation resource management at Slippery Rock University in May 1998. She is currently working on her M.A. degree in park administration at Central Michigan University, where she is a graduate assistant. Holly has held several seasonal recreation positions including recreation supervisor, environmental camp counselor, museum guide, and park ranger. Upon completion of her master's degree, Holly hopes to obtain a position as a park manager.

FOREWORD

We invite you to explore the exciting and remarkably diverse professional career opportunities that are available in the field of recreation and leisure services. There has never been a more exciting time to become involved in the profession. Today we are increasingly a leisure-oriented society. The average full-time employee works fewer than forty hours a week. A third of our time is spent in leisure. Americans spend about a third of their income on leisure pursuits. One-third of our land is donated to leisure and recreation and more than two-thirds of Americans perceive that their leisure is of equal or greater importance to them than their work. Increasingly, we measure the quality of our lives by the satisfactions derived from our leisure experiences. As a result, jobs are plentiful, and continued growth in career opportunities can be expected in the next decades.

Professional careers in recreation and leisure services offer challenging, meaningful, and highly rewarding opportunities in human services. Whether your interests are in working with children, teens, adults, or seniors; with outdoor adventure, cultural arts, sports, or social activities; or in hospital/clinical settings, theme parks, or the military, recreation and leisure services offers job opportunities for you.

We invite you to consider a career in the profession of recreation and leisure services. You will have the satisfaction of enjoying your work and an opportunity to make unique and significant contributions to the quality of life of those you serve.

Good luck with your careers.

> Roger L. Coles, Ed.D.
> Department Chair, Recreation
> Central Michigan University
> and
> Christen G. Smith, Ph.D.
> Faculty
> Aurora University (Illinois)

PREFACE

Leisure time occupations are among the most rapidly growing vocations in America. The recreation industry has been and is currently preparing for a leisure-oriented society, and the field of recreational leadership is steadily becoming a well-established profession. Consequently there has been an upsurge in career opportunities and career preparation programs in leisure-related fields.

Serving an industry that annually exceeds $150 billion in expenditures, trained workers in a variety of occupations are involved in the provision of leisure services. Visualize, for example, the variety of jobs and the number of people involved in the design and production of sporting and recreation equipment, the provision of all sorts of recreation services, facility planning and construction, program planning, and direct recreation leadership. Further, commercial entertainment establishments, travel agencies, professional sports organizations, outdoor recreation producers, and many other such services are very much a part of the exploding leisure market. Indeed, leisure services in total involve a multitude of business and professional activities that employ millions of people.

Since it would be impractical to cover all of the leisure occupations, the content of this book is limited to the recreation and park profession and certain closely related fields. Unlike many areas of employment that face the threat of diminishing importance because of technology and automation, this interesting occupational field will offer expanding opportunities in both the near- and long-term future.

ACKNOWLEDGMENTS

I would like to thank two people for the opportunity to revise this book, Roger Coles and Peggy Gisler, who put their faith in me to get the job done. Also, a big thank you goes out to my co-workers who have seen me through my first book revision attempt. The support and assistance of all of these individuals has been invaluable.

H.B.

CHAPTER 1

RECREATION FOR THE NEW MILLENNIUM

Leisure is the best of all possessions.

Socrates

As we approach the twenty-first century, thanks to modern technology, increased vacation time, flexible work schedules, and early retirement many people are able to start enjoying more recreation and leisure time now than in any other period in our history. People today are spending their leisure time doing recreational activities like in-line skating, snowboarding, and hang gliding that our grandparents never even dreamed would exist.

What do you enjoy doing during your leisure time? Housework? Research at the library? Painting the gutters? Grocery shopping? Not on your life! When we think of how we want to spend our leisure time, we usually think of doing activities labeled "recreation." Hiking, golf, tennis, and camping are all recreational activities that people enjoy doing in their leisure time. In the minds of most people, recreation and the use of leisure time are synonymous. It is important to recognize, however, that there are many uses of leisure that are not recreative.

The word *recreation* is derived from the Latin word *recreare,* which means "to create anew, to become refreshed." The dictionary further defines the term as "the refreshment of strength or spirit, revigoration or rebirth." Recreation is essentially a "renewing" experience—a refreshing change from work and the daily routine.

If we accept the idea that recreation actually recreates the participant, then many so-called recreation pursuits are not recreation at all. They are only amusers, time fillers, and time wasters, some of which fatigue rather than rejuvenate, "decreate" rather than recreate, and actually deprive participants of enrichment opportunities vital to their development and fulfillment.

In his book *Philosophy of Recreation and Leisure,* J. B. Nash added meaning to the quality concept of recreation by placing different kinds of pursuits into a hierarchy on the basis of their potential value to the individual and society. Figure 1 is a modified version of Nash's original interpretation.

The deeper meaning of recreation goes beyond amusement and hobby. It includes activities of the highest order of creative, cultural, and civic values that enrich our lives and elevate the tone of society. Clear understanding of this broader concept among recreation professionals and community leaders is critical because it is a fundamental concept that is already lagging well behind.

The term *recreation* implies that the participant is recreated physically, psychologically, spiritually, or mentally; that he or she becomes refreshed and enriched; that he or she is revitalized and more ready to cope with the routines and trials of life. True recreation is clearly distinguished from simple amusements and time fillers because true recreation provides an experience of quality to the participant.

Recreational activities take many forms and must be suited to an individual's particular needs and interests. People enjoy fish-

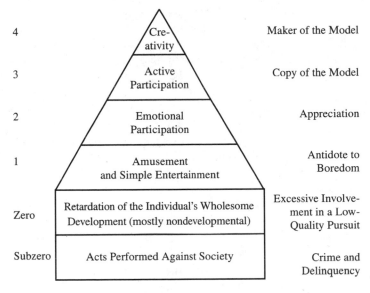

Figure 1

ing, skiing, singing, photography, dancing, playing a guitar, swimming, or going to a good play; nevertheless, one person's recreation may be another's drudgery. Building a boat, for example, can be an ideal leisure activity to one person, whereas to another it would be work. Even with the same individual an activity that is recreational at one time or under certain conditions does not always yield satisfaction that makes it recreation. Sometimes a person feels like playing golf or participating in a square dance group; at other times he or she prefers a very different form of involvement. When a person is physically fatigued, there is little need for vigorous physical recreation. When mentally or emotionally fatigued, a person is not attracted to activities that require heavy concentration. Recreation usually takes the form of diversion and helps to bring one's life into balance. To some the park is a place to play. To others it is for beauty, meditation, and study of nature. Further, some people want to preserve nature's resources in order to enjoy them in their present state, while others see little value to them unless they are used to produce material goods. An important task of those involved in leisure time occupations is to sense the needs and interests of different people and to supply facilities, programs, and leadership that will be appealing and satisfying.

There is a real danger in placing too much emphasis on looking and listening as recreation. Very often this kind of involvement is no more than a time filler; however, there is a spectator level that may be creative. When an individual goes to a great concert, sees a painting, hears a pianist, sees great athletes in performance, or sees the performance or products of people in whom he or she has special interest, there may be a beneficial level of emotional participation or a creative result. The observer may say, "That's what I would like to have said," or "That is what I believe." Seeing such performances or products sometimes lifts one to a higher level, so that standing before Michelangelo's statue of "David" or Rodin's "Thinker," or any appealing work of art, or attending a worthy performance may cause the appreciative person to want to live better and accomplish more. Sometimes seeing and listening provides a model that results in improvement, and sometimes it arouses a level of appreciation, even though the spectator is unable to follow the model or has no desire to do so. However, the danger of spectatorism is that people will simply be amused and pacified hour after hour, and this may actually destroy motivation and opportunity to do something more developmental and worthy.

THE TOTAL RECREATION EXPERIENCE

At first, a recreation experience may appear to be confined to the block of time during which participation actually occurs. But, upon further analysis, it becomes apparent that the total experience extends far beyond the time of actual participation. The value and usefulness of the experience may be part of a person's life long before, and remain long after, the participation itself. A total recreation experience includes the following four phases: anticipation, planning, participation, and recollection.

The *anticipation phase* is that time during which the person foresees the greatness of the coming event—the time of eagerly awaiting the day when the experience will become a reality. It is during this time that enthusiasm starts to develop. This phase includes the anticipation of catching a big trout, climbing a high mountain, bagging another deer, elk, or moose; the thought of next summer's canoe trip, learning to ski, or riding horseback. Some "would-be" recreation events never progress beyond the anticipation phase, but even then they make some contributions to one's life. Sometimes this phase extends over a long period and often stimulates some reading and study and much conversation.

The *planning phase* involves the actual preparation for the coming event—the gathering of equipment and supplies, preparation of food and clothes, travel arrangements, and other such necessary matters. If done well, this can be an educational experience and sometimes is a social event.

The *participation phase* is the period of the actual activity and the duration of the event. It extends from the time of departure until the time of return. Often this phase is relatively short as compared to the other phases, and it may seem almost insignificant in terms of time. Yet it is the core around which the other three phases are built. This is the actual experience of fishing, hunting, canoeing, swimming, camping, boating, skiing, hiking, or whatever the activity may be.

The *recollection phase* may take the form of thought, expression in oral or written form, or the displaying of pictures, slides, and movies. This phase is the thinking, telling, and showing about the direct experiences that have occurred. Fortunately, there is no time limit for this phase.

Sometimes anticipation, planning, and recollection are more exciting than the participation itself, but it takes all four phases to make the recreational experience complete. None of the four phases should be downplayed in terms of its potential contributions.

AN IMPORTANT CHALLENGE

Parks and recreation professionals are facing many challenges as we enter the new millennium. Their job is to provide relief for people from the stressful environments they live in. They play a vital role in people living healthier and happier lives. As communities become more diverse, parks and recreation professionals must continually re-examine their approach to recreation so they are able to meet the changing needs of the citizens they serve. Not only will they be challenged by youth in at-risk environments and individuals wanting high-risk adventures such as bungee jumping, skydiving, and mountain climbing, but they will be challenged to keep up with technological advances. Computers are no longer the strict domain of accountants and engineers. Computers are in schools and grocery stores and play a complex role in park and recreation facilities.

The emphasis on computer literacy continues to increase in parks and recreation. Employees working in these fields must be able to use computers and statistical techniques to help them assess, plan, and evaluate. The new millennium facing the parks and recreation professionals looks bright provided they place no boundaries or limitations on the challenges that the twenty-first century brings to their profession. They must also face the fact that another basic problem associated with increased leisure time is that it does not guarantee better individuals or an improved society. It requires the making of choices, and to ensure wise choices, the recreation and leisure fields must provide both adequate education and good leadership. Leaders in the recreation and park field must help to provide people with positive alternatives and with the background to make the right choices.

Americans have not yet proved that abundant leisure can be used beneficially. The "leisure era" is still in the development stage, and the outcome is certainly in question. There are some bright aspects of the leisure trend caused by perceptive and responsible people who have stood ready to add quality and meaning to life through challenging and enriching leisure pursuits. However, there is also a segment of the population that has seriously abused its newfound treasure, even to the point of using it for pursuits that are degrading. Society must deal with the fundamental problem that abundant leisure is neither inherently good or bad, but has tremendous potential for either. Leisure activities are, however, able to provide new opportunities for people to make choices.

DEALING WITH THE MISCONCEPTIONS

With the large number of books and articles that have been written during recent years on leisure and recreation, a number of misconceptions have arisen. It is important to identify these misconceptions and try to correct or avoid them.

1. It is often thought that recreation is strictly the antithesis of work. This is a misconception. It is true that for many people the

hours of employment are repetitive, boring, and exhausting. Today relatively few people find recreation in their work, but there are some individuals who do.

2. Leisure time and recreation are frequently treated as though they are essentially the same or inseparable. This is not totally correct. It is true that in most instances opportunities for recreation are confined to leisure hours. Therefore, recreation is primarily a leisure time activity. However, not all leisure time is spent in recreational pursuits. Much of it is wasted or occupied with activities that do not have recreative results. Leisure time can be filled either with true recreation or with low grade amusers, time wasters, or "decreative" activities.

3. Some people stress the concept that recreation must be earned by doing useful work. This would imply that recreation is not essential of itself and is not viewed as an end; instead, it is a sort of recuperative interlude between periods of work. It fails to recognize the significant nature and vital purpose of recreation itself—a desirable state of being, whether in preparation for work or not.

4. Some see recreation only as therapeutic in nature; as a means of solving or alleviating personal and community problems. In fact, a recreational experience is likely to bring greater satisfaction to an individual if it also contributes to the individual's personal development and to the betterment of his or her community.

5. To think of recreation as specific activities is a misconception. Even though certain activities frequently yield pleasurable experiences to a large number of people, they are merely means of achieving recreation and are not recreation themselves. Recreation is a result, not an activity.

6. Another misconception is that recreation, unlike education, is essentially without purpose or discipline. This misunderstand-

ing occurs because recreation is identified with relaxation or pleasurable involvement. In many forms of recreation there is a high degree of concentration, physical exertion, and mental application. Some forms are stimulating and enriching while other forms are keenly challenging and press the participants almost to their limits. These forms of recreation certainly result in individual development.

ARE YOU SUITED TO THE CHALLENGE?

You must be someone who enjoys your recreation and leisure time to be reading this book and considering a full-time career organizing and directing activities that will meet the physical and mental needs of a diverse group of people. However, before you jump into the field, take the time to ask yourself the following questions to make sure you are really on the path of your dream career.

Do you enjoy working with people?

Do you enjoy the outdoor experience?

Are you able to work with a diverse group of people?

Do you have the ability to lead?

Are you knowledgeable about recreational activities and equipment?

Do you enjoy participating in athletic programs?

Do you have the ability to help people find the recreational activity to meet their needs?

Can you teach adults and children?

Are you able to provide guidance and supervision in recreational activities?

Are you a quick thinker?

Can you handle a crisis situation?

Can you get a diverse group of people involved in one activity?

Do you enjoy leisure activities in all types of weather?

Do you mind working more than forty hours a week?

Are you flexible enough to work a diverse schedule?

If you were able to respond positively to most of the questions above, then you should continue reading this book because in Chapter 2 you will learn about current occupations in the field that are needed to meet society's demands. Then Chapter 3 will be helpful as it discusses the trends affecting employment today. Chapter 4 will tell you the characteristics and essential professional goals you must have in the recreation and leisure field. If you are really serious about finding a career in recreation and leisure, then Chapter 5 will prove invaluable because it goes into great detail about the educational training you will need and exactly what schools offer programs that you might be interested in enough to research further. Chapter 6 will give you tips on where to find a job. And in Chapter 7 you will enjoy reading personal stories of people out working in the field that you are now seriously considering. Chapter 8 gives you a list of organizations that can provide you with more information about recreation and leisure careers, and membership in some might help you enhance your future career. Chapter 9 gives you an overview of how recreation and leisure careers are keeping up with the times and what you can expect in the future. Finally Appendixes A and B will provide you with federal and state agencies, and potential employing organizations.

Opportunities for employment in parks and recreation vary greatly from one facility to another. You could work out in the field as a park ranger, be involved in the planning and programming of activities, or even be in a main office as a recreation administrator at recreation areas ranging from community park systems to national parks. All of these positions and facilities and many, many more would provide their own challenges and satisfactions for someone working in the recreation and leisure field.

CHAPTER 2

OCCUPATIONS TO MEET
SOCIETY'S DEMANDS

> How we Americans spend leisure time might seem to
> have little bearing on the strength of our nation or the worth
> and prestige of our free society. Yet we certainly cannot
> continue to thrive as a strong and vigorous free people
> unless we understand and use creatively one of our greatest
> resources—our leisure.
>
> John F. Kennedy

The variety of leisure time activities is continually increasing as
the number of people devoting their careers to leisure time occupations is on the rise. Leisure time occupations refer to various
jobs that people engage in to provide opportunities for other people during leisure hours. These leisure time occupations are
numerous and diverse.

The following list of titles or positions represents a sampling of
today's recreation and leisure service careers. We can't be sure
what the new millennium will produce, but one can rest assured
that possibilities for recreation careers will grow.

Aquatics program director
Aquatics specialist
Armed forces recreation leader

Camp counselor
Camp director
Campground attendant
Carnival game operator
Church recreation director
College professor
Commercial game center director
Community center director
Community development specialist
Community education worker
Concert promoter
Concessionaire
Condominium social director
Cruise ship activity director
Dance instructor
Environmental interpreter
Facility designer
Facility operator
Fisheries conservationist
Fitness specialist
Forester
Game protector
Golf pro
High-rise recreation facilitator
Industrial recreation specialist
Leisure counselor
Leisure education specialist
Municipal recreation leader
Museum guide
Naturalist
Outdoor and waterway guide
Outdoor recreation manager

Outfitter
Park ranger
Park superintendent
Playground leader
Prison recreation specialist
Recreation facility manager
Recreation therapist
Resort manager
River guide
Senior citizen programmer
Ski instructor
Special populations programmer
Tennis pro
Therapeutic recreation specialist
Tour guide
Travel planner
Volunteer agency supervisor
Wilderness trip guide
Wildlife biologist
Wildlife conservationist
Youth agency recreator
Youth sports coach
Zoological and botanical garden director

Many of these occupations are naturals for people who are highly skilled athletes or entertainers, especially if they have reputations that will attract clientele. Such persons might become golf pros, tennis or ski instructors, or summer theater directors. The particular curricula that such persons pursue in college is sometimes of limited importance—reputation, personality, and expertise are more important in attracting a clientele. However, for most recreation leadership positions, the best avenue is through a college program in some aspect of recreation and park management that prepares one to assume a professional position and to advance as the opportunities come along. It is for these people that experience is often the key.

DIVISIONS OF RECREATION

The recreation field has been logically divided into four groups: *recreation services, recreation resources, tourism,* and *amusement and entertainment.*

The *recreation services* group involves leadership in organized recreational activities. This includes creating and supervising programs, planning activities, and providing leadership and instruction. These leisure time experiences take place in a variety of settings—parks, playgrounds, camps, community centers—and involve a great deal of personal interaction.

The *recreation resources* group includes jobs relating to the planning, development, maintenance, and protection of resources, both natural and man-made, used for leisure time activities. These jobs deal with recreational areas and facilities, and, in a sense, they form a support system for recreational experiences.

The *tourism group* includes jobs related to travel for pleasure (rather than for business or duty) and activities for tourists. Within this group are five major components: attracting a market for tourism; providing transportation to places of interest; providing attractions for tourist participation; housing, feeding, and serving tourists; and informing people about attractions, services, facilities, and transportation, then making specific arrangements for them.

Occupations in amusement and entertainment include jobs to entertain clientele, including commercial amusements; live or filmed performances; presentation of shows and professional athletic contests; and personal services in entertainment establishments.

It is apparent that the first two groups of occupations (recreation services and recreation resources) constitute the more professional portion of this occupational field. These two groups would employ those who pursue a college education in preparation for leisure time occupations.

In addition to the people working in the four categories described above, the leisure-oriented fields support a number of other occupations. These include people involved in the construction of facilities and areas; commercial establishments, such as stores, shops, and service stations, located at or near major parks and resorts; and industries involved in the production of a great variety of recreation equipment—athletic gear, boats and motors, and fishing and hunting equipment. There are numerous other occupations that depend either completely or partly upon people's leisure time pursuits. It is apparent that if leisure time were suddenly eliminated, a major portion of the economy would suffer significant damage, and a very large number of people in a variety of occupations would become unemployed.

New developments in technology affect the demand for recreational services. For example, modern mechanical lifts have revolutionized skiing, and innovations in snow-making equipment have made skiing quite popular in moderate temperature zones. Dam building and reservoir developments by the U.S. Army Corps of Engineers, the Bureau of Reclamation, and other agencies, coupled with mass production of boats and marine equipment, have contributed toward a dramatic increase in water sports. Golf may be significantly affected by a new computerized golf game utilizing limited space.

In travel and tourism, we are on the horizon of new dimensions. A short time ago the first tourist excursion was taken to the Antarctic, an area where only exploration parties had gone previously. In the future, tourist excursions under the sea and into outer space are certainly promising possibilities.

DEVELOPMENT OF THE RECREATION PROFESSION

The earliest city park in the United States was the Boston Commons, established in 1634. When in 1682 William Penn laid out Philadelphia, he included in his plan numerous small parks and ornamental plots. In his 1791 plan for Washington, DC, Pierre Charles L'Enfant provided spacious public parks, squares, fountains, walks, and broad, tree-lined avenues. Squares, commons, and village greens had become numerous in the New England states by the early nineteenth century.

Quite separate from the city park movement, municipal recreation programming was born out of social conscience. It grew up with the settlement house, kindergarten, and youth movements that fostered the great youth agencies of the nation. Its earliest practitioners were motivated by human welfare; the social ends of human development, suppression of juvenile delinquency, informal education, cultural enrichment, health improvement, and other similar objectives were central.

Certain events of the late nineteenth century brought about the realization that there was a growing need for new and different kinds of leisure time opportunities. A rapidly changing industrialized society, along with the advancement of science, more formal education, increased population and urbanization, and changing social attitudes, had immediate effects on leisure time and its uses.

During the 1820s and 1830s, a new trend emerged when several outdoor gymnasiums were built in Massachusetts and New York.

In 1853, New York City acquired Central Park—the first time any city in the United States set aside public land strictly for leisure purposes. During the second half of the century, numerous cities followed New York's example and acquired large tracts of land for parks.

The first record of anyone being employed in a leisure time occupation, other than those who planned parks, was in 1885 when several women were hired as supervisors for children's playgrounds in Boston. In 1898, New York City opened thirty-one supervised playgrounds under the direction of the state board of education, and, soon after that, the city moved quickly to develop a large network of playgrounds paid for and administered by the city government. Further, all schools in the city were required to have open air playgrounds. By the end of the nineteenth century, at least fourteen American cities had made provisions for supervised public recreation facilities.

At about the same time, the settlement house movement was underway, spreading rapidly in densely populated areas. These social settlements had many of the same characteristics as today's community recreation centers.

The first metropolitan park system was established in Boston in 1892, and the first county system was organized in Essex County, New Jersey, in 1895. The New England Association of Park Superintendents (later known as the American Institute of Park Executives) was organized in 1898. By the turn of the century, the pattern for the recreation and park movement was well established.

The basis of this new movement was essentially social. Its early advocates pointed to such evils as dangerous streets, delinquency, unsanitary living conditions, child labor, congestion of cities, and lack of space for play and rest. They declared that the individual should be the center of the educational effort and that activities during leisure were important to the person's overall development.

Chicago's South Park Playground System developed during the early 1900s, and these playgrounds, with their carefully planned field houses and spacious outdoor areas, had significant influence on the recreation movement. This concept represented a milestone in the public's responsibility for facilities and paid leadership. The concept spread quickly into Rochester, Boston, and Los Angeles.

By 1906 the recreation and park movement had gained such support that at a meeting in Washington, DC, of park and playground promoters, a new organization was founded, known as the Playground Association of America, which later became the National Recreation Association (1917), and still later the National Recreation and Park Association (1965). Joseph Lee, a Harvard law graduate and wealthy philanthropist, was president of the association for twenty-seven years. Lee argued that play was a serious activity in children's social adjustment and that recreation had vital significance for everyone who wanted a meaningful life. Lee emphasized quality experiences and advocated the need for fixed goals, efficient organization, and expert leadership. He advocated education for the wise use of leisure as the means to helping people achieve happy and creative lives.

Although disruptive to the development of recreation in some respects, both World Wars actually contributed markedly to the movement. Men in the service were being exposed to well-organized recreational services. Further, many civilians clustered in industrial centers where they also were exposed to organized recreation. Following each World War, soldiers and civilians carried back to their own communities the desire to provide better organized programs.

During the period between the two wars the country became increasingly industrialized and highly mobile. These two characteristics had dramatic influences on the amount and kinds of leisure time activities engaged in by Americans.

Following World War II, with the American economy at its highest level in history and with the return of large numbers of soldiers and defense workers to their hometowns, practically every community of any size initiated some sort of community recreation program. In most cases the program was sponsored by the local government and supported from tax funds. It was during this period that the municipal recreation and park movement erupted into a nationwide trend.

Concurrently and subsequently, other agencies gave additional attention to people's leisure time needs. Voluntary youth serving agencies became more concerned about the recreational needs of their members, and at industrial plants employee recreation associations developed. The armed forces also continued to provide recreational opportunities for their members, and uses of the out-of-doors for recreational purposes skyrocketed. During the postwar years commercial recreation enjoyed its greatest boom, and, more recently, specialized programs of recreation therapy for persons with disabilities have become popular.

Modern technology has revolutionized certain leisure time pursuits. For example motorboating, waterskiing, snow skiing, scuba diving, driving for pleasure, tourist travel, modern camping, video games, and numerous other forms of recreation have been influenced greatly by technological advances.

Further, television has had a significant influence through mass exposure of activities that would otherwise remain relatively unexposed. Over the past decade, we have seen major increases in some activities, while others have decreased. Some of the largest increases were in snowboarding, in-line skating, and step aerobics. Some of the biggest decreases were in windsurfing, tennis, and racquetball. Overall, though, more people are taking advantage of recreation activities and the decrease in one activity is made up for with an increase in others.

Because of the steady escalation of leisure time and recreational participation, there are now numerous leisure time job opportunities at every level of public agencies (especially the local level), in volunteer organizations, and with private and commercial enterprises. For the most part, the jobs are specialized, requiring people with certain personality characteristics and specific competencies. Because of the great variety of agencies and activities involved, there is a good chance that an interesting and challenging leisure time occupation could await you.

CHAPTER 3

TRENDS AFFECTING EMPLOYMENT

UNDERLYING FORCES OF CHANGE

In recent decades, it seems that as soon as we get used to the latest change, it is replaced by yet another. Many of these changes relate to leisure and create a need for flexible professionals. This "new breed" of professionals needs to have adequate preparation and leadership in leisure time activities. Changes that have happened and will have such influences are the following:

Work and Leisure. Work and leisure are the two sides of our shields. The one side, labor, enables us to live while the other side, leisure, makes living more meaningful.

The average workweek in America in 1850 was almost 70 hours; in 1900 it was 55 hours; and by 1950 it had been reduced to about 40 hours. Some occupational groups are now on workweeks of fewer than 40 hours. Economic and labor specialists predict that in the near future Americans will average only 36 hours of work per week.

While the workweek becomes shorter, weekends and vacation periods become longer, and people are retiring at an earlier age. When we sum up all these trends, it is apparent that Americans today spend significantly more time at leisure than ever before.

The total amount of leisure tells only part of the story; distribution of time and the size of its increments are other important factors. *Daily leisure* comes in segments of one to several hours following a day of labor. *Weekly leisure* is defined in terms of weekends, many of which will be three days in the future. *Annual vacation* time represents a longer period that the worker has earned by a year of labor.

The average American now lives to an age of about seventy-five, with women living an average of about six years longer than men. Most people reaching retirement age will have a substantial block of time on their hands, and some of them will have two or three decades.

The cumulative effect of the gradual increases in the forms of leisure will certainly have a significant impact on the amount of choosing time that people will have in the future. In turn, this will have a marked effect on the kinds of recreational opportunities that will need to be provided.

It is interesting that time, whether it is involved with work or leisure, cannot be stored or saved or consumed at a rate faster than it is produced. Rich people have no more time than poor people and no less. Like all other forms of time, leisure must be consumed either by doing something or doing nothing.

Some people become slaves of their own possessions instead of creative users of their leisure. All of us know a neighbor or friend whose material goods for leisure (boats, campers, snowmobiles, skiing equipment, vacation homes) are so extensive that their lives are dominated by trying to pay for them. For some, the pleasure appears to be in possessing and not in the joy of participation.

It is obvious that even with an abundance of leisure and with the promise of still more to come, each of us must still be highly selective about how we use leisure time or else it will not serve its best purpose. Leisure can be a great blessing, but to some it becomes a kind of curse due to boredom, participation in poorly selected activities, or overindulgence of one kind or another.

Changing Philosophy. Leisure and recreation traditionally have been viewed with suspicion, while work has been held as one of the highest values of American life. Moreover, work traditionally has been associated with more than material accomplishments; it has been a source of social and moral recognition.

Even though contemporary concepts do not, and should not, minimize the values of work, they do express greater appreciation for leisure and participation in wholesome recreational pursuits. People today realize that wholesome recreation contributes to one's personality and adds to life a spirit of adventure, creativity, and enrichment.

The fundamental truth that recreation is essential to the cultural, moral, and spiritual well-being of people in a society such as ours has been reaffirmed. The challenge to use leisure time effectively and constructively demands full development of local, state, and national resources and requires a sufficient amount of high quality leadership.

Automation. Even though some people argue that automation at worst simply changes people's occupations and at best creates additional jobs, the facts presented by industrial leaders and the United States Department of Labor indicate that several thousand jobs per week are eliminated in the United States as a result of automation. This condition is partly counterbalanced by spreading the jobs out on a thinner base, as evidenced by the fact that more than seven-hundred United States companies have all or most of their workers on a four-day workweek, and at least one thousand other companies are contemplating such a shift. In 1973, the nation's largest employer, the federal government, began to experiment with the four-day workweek, as did the municipalities of Atlanta, Long Beach, and Phoenix. A dozen companies, including

Metropolitan Life Insurance, have gone even further, assigning some of their workers to a three-day week on an experimental basis.

Some experts believe that automation has only begun its replacement of people; they believe that within the next two decades we shall see an unprecedented rise in unemployment among the skilled and middle management groups as well as the uneducated. They predict a society where a smaller percentage of the population will provide the basic necessities for all. If these predictions are realized, then truly one of the greatest needs in America will be a large number of well-prepared people in the various leisure time occupations. The provision of enriching and uplifting leisure time activities will become fundamental to a strong society and high-quality living.

Population. Both the number and the distribution of people influence the amount and kinds of opportunities and leadership that are needed. It is interesting that worldwide approximately 220 babies are born each minute while about 140 people die. In other words, if your heart rate is normal (72 beats per minute), about three people are added while two people die with each beat of your heart. At this rate the world's population increases each week by about .73 million.

The United States's population almost doubled from 1900 to 1950, an increase from 85 million to 151 million. Then during the next forty years (1950 to 1990), it increased another 89 million, bringing the total to 240 million. Currently the United States is growing at a rate of about 3 million people per year. In percentage, the increase is lower than it has ever been, but in numbers the rate is still very dramatic.

Another interesting characteristic of population is age distribution. A male child born in 1900 could expect to live 46 years whereas one born in 1990 has a life expectancy of 74 years. For females, the gain has been even greater; from 48 years in 1900 to

79 years in 1990. What will life expectancy increase to in the new millennium?

In 1940, 25 percent of the population was 15 and under; by 1990 this figure had increased to 35 percent. In 1940, 10 percent of the population was age 60 or more; by 1990 that percentage had reached 19 percent. The proportion of both young and old members of the population (nonworking ages) is increasing steadily.

Of course, the population in the United States does not live in isolation from the rest of the world. Therefore population trends worldwide are important to know about.

Most of the world's human population lives in underdeveloped countries or in countries where the natural resources are nearly depleted. This factor—of large, poverty-stricken populations—contributes to social unrest and political instability and smothers efforts to develop better lives by the millions of people who are ill-fed, ill-clothed, ill-housed, poorly educated, and who lack the basic requirements of an enriched life.

North America and western Europe presently have about 17 percent of the world's population and 64 percent of the income as measured in goods and services produced. Asia has 56 percent of the population and 14 percent of the income. The deprived and underprivileged portion of the population is increasing more rapidly than the affluent portion.

It has been calculated that if the present rate of population growth had existed since the beginning of the Christian era, we would now have an average of one square yard of earth for each living person. That would hardly be enough for breathing room, much less mountain climbing, skiing, and long golf drives. Further, it has been calculated that if the present rate of increase continues, the earth's resources will simply not be able to sustain the population.

Urbanization. The number of people living in a given area (density) influences their living patterns. More people mean more residential and industrial areas and more streets, parking lots, schools, and shopping centers, all at the expense of shrinking natural spaces.

Technology. Visualize the amount of human energy that would be needed to propel an automobile 60 m.p.h. for just one mile. Further, visualize the human effort that it would take to generate and deliver the electricity for running our refrigerators, disposals, electric lights, and heating or air-conditioning units over a 24-hour period. Think of the thousands of hours that would be spent making calculations that can be accomplished on a computer in just 30 seconds. Even more impressive is the equivalent energy spent on a four-engine jetliner streaking through space at 600 m.p.h. or a 100-car freight train traveling at 50 m.p.h.

These technologized time- and energy-saving items are largely responsible for the increased leisure that is presently available. At the same time other technical devices influence how we use our leisure in recreational pursuits. For example, powerboating and waterskiing are new found pleasures that depend directly upon technology. The same is true for downhill skiing, underwater motorized exploration, driving for pleasure, and recreation involving aircraft and off-road vehicles. Many other recreational pursuits are influenced less directly but substantially by the availability of electricity, better modes of travel to and from locations, and new and better implements and objects involved in our varied forms of participation such as sports implements and hunting and fishing gear.

Technology experts predict that we shall make more technological progress in the next twenty years than was made in any equivalent period of the past. A generation of computers is coming along fast without waiting for the rest of us to deal with the wholesale changes that will result. The computers of the future will be fast enough to do a decade of work during a lunch hour and their impact will be felt not only by blue collar workers but by skillful technicians and management personnel as well. Further, American scientists can see real possibilities for developing electric automobiles, nonpetroleum aircraft fuel, abundant solar energy units for heating, and a host of other new timesaving and energy-saving devices. Also, significant strides will continue toward improved household implements, making household management less time consuming.

A technologist is truly a significant contributor to our lifestyle—both on and off the job. Technological advances will give us significantly more choosing time in the future and more alternatives to choose from. As a result, technology will contribute to leisure time job opportunities and will also help influence the nature of these jobs.

Mobility. Possibly the most distinctive feature of life in America is its mobility. Whether we travel by land, air, or sea for long or short distances, comfortable and rapid transportation is available. Our most common mode by far is the automobile, followed respectively by air, train, and boat travel. At the present time the entire U.S. population could be seated comfortably in their privately owned cars, and the average would be only about 2.5 persons per car.

Even though the automobile is still our primary means of travel, other transportation modes have become increasingly important. Air passengers increased from 2.5 million in 1940 to an estimated 90 million in 1990. The six-hundred-mile-per-hour jetliner has revolutionized air travel and has put all parts of the nation within a day's travel. In a sense the nation will take to the air in the future. Our remarkable mobility will afford people in large numbers the opportunity to spend more of their increased leisure time in areas of their choice, and this will have significant effects on people's recreational patterns.

Education. There has been an awakening of average citizens, Jane and John Doe, to the fact that a high level of education is essential if they are to live effectively in our complex society. As a result, not only has the total number of students greatly increased, so has the average level of education. In 1910, only 63 percent of school-age children (five to eighteen years) were enrolled in school. By 1930, this percentage was 72, and it is presently around 88 percent.

A greater number of students are going on to college. College enrollments increased from 2.5 million in 1950 to 3.2 million in 1960, and 6 million in 1970. The present college enrollment exceeds 13.2 million. The great move toward a college education is further demonstrated by the fact that in the early 1950s only 27 percent of college age students were enrolled in college while this number has now reached about 45 percent.

This increased attention to education has two startling effects on planning for recreation. First, education is the key to higher personal income, and higher income influences what people do for recreation and where they go to do it. Second, as people further their education they tend to broaden their horizon of interests, appreciations, and skills in recreation pursuits. Therefore, educated people tend not only to have more varied recreational interests but also more means with which to pursue them.

Income. Today's consumers are more than two-and-one-half times better off than the consumers in the mid-1930s and 18 percent better off than consumers in the best economic years during World War II. American consumers today have more purchasing power than ever before.

Based on the recent past, it is safe to assume that in the future people will spend more on hobbies, sports, adventure, and other recreation that provides increased satisfaction. Many will own two homes, one of which will be in a resort area. Two-car families will become three-car families, and the cars will be used more for pleasure than necessity. Boats, camping equipment, athletic gear, hunting and fishing supplies, ski equipment, hobby supplies, and other recreational goods and services will be purchased in ever-increasing amounts. In the coming years leisure activities will capture an even greater amount of the individual's income and will contribute increasingly to the nation's economy.

Environmental Crisis. The quality of the environment will continue to be a major issue. The sight of natural beauty, the breathing of clean air, and the availability of clear, pure water are becoming rare to many Americans because the environment in many areas has become degraded and polluted. It is difficult if not impossible for people to have satisfying and enriching outdoor experiences under such conditions. One of the important contributions of people in leisure time occupations is their real concern for the environment and their leadership in improving conditions.

Overcrowded Facilities. In populated areas, overcrowded parks, playgrounds, and swimming pools are not uncommon, and these conditions will become even more common in the absence of adequate leadership. Often in areas where recreation facilities are inadequate, people seem willing to spend their money on such nonproductive expenditures as the overuse of automobiles, the purchase of unnecessary gadgets, and drinking, smoking, and overeating. As part of the educational process as it relates to leisure time, people need to learn that adequate facilities for enriching and developmental activities are far more important than some of the amusement activities on which people presently squander money. This educational process involves development of a sound set of values relating to life in general and to leisure time activities in particular.

Violence and Social Unrest. Demonstrations of unrest and violence and the apparent underlying causes are matters that should be of concern to all responsible citizens and particularly to those involved in planning of leisure time activities. Some of these problems can be avoided, and many of them can be at least partially solved through the provision of an adequate amount of satisfying leisure time opportunities. Certainly leisure time programs do not offer the total solution to such problems, but those in leisure time occupations can make a significant contribution toward some constructive solutions.

CHAPTER 4

CHARACTERISTICS AND ESSENTIAL PROFESSIONAL GOALS

The new millennium brings with it a new perspective and liberation from the past. We find ourselves in an environment of new opportunity for personal enrichment. We are now more free to think, feel, and exercise impulses without worrying about the bare essentials of survival. We are in an age of not realizing the need that our forefathers felt.

In order to take advantage of this circumstance, the average American must be taught how to use leisure time to its fullest potential.

Leaders are needed to teach people this valuable knowledge and lead them in leisure pursuits. On top of the leaders who work directly with the people, professionals are needed to help on a larger scale. These skillful individuals will communicate purposes and appreciations, encourage the installation of adequate facilities, and accept the responsibility for cultural initiative and the development of cultural traditions. It is a combination of these two types of professionals that allows large numbers of people to achieve enrichment.

PERSONAL REQUIREMENTS

While highly specialized jobs require their own particular individual characteristics, there are some personal traits that are essential for any leadership position in the recreational field. Any person who contemplates entering the field should read these carefully and think about himself or herself with respect to them:

- Ability to work effectively with members of the public of various ages and backgrounds.
- Insight into the kinds of leisure time opportunities people need to round out their lives and achieve fulfillment.
- A sound sense of values on which accurate and appropriate decisions and leadership efforts will be based.
- A range of skills, interests, and appreciations to which people should and will devote their leisure time.
- A sincere interest in public service and the positive development of individuals and society.
- The specific knowledge and skills necessary for his or her particular kind of work. For example, an administrator of a recreation program must possess the same basic administrative skills as a school administrator or a manager of a business while a designer of recreational facilities must possess the same kinds of competencies as other designers, and a teacher of leisure time activities must be competent by standards comparable to other teachers.
- A personable individual whom members of the public will respect and look toward for leadership.
- A cooperative attitude and a dedication to cooperation among individuals and agencies involved in leisure time pursuits.
- Common sense that will help in understanding and dealing with people and with situations.
- The ability to enjoy life and to cause others to do the same.

Park and recreation professionals must continue their progress toward overcoming their long-time public image of "playground babysitters" or "public groundkeepers." Their responsibilities are too great for this image to continue. They must enhance their image by improving their qualifications as executives, innovators, planners, teachers, supervisors, and leaders of broad and complex leisure-oriented programs of real quality and meaning.

Further, park and recreation professionals must be competent in working with various kinds of natural and man-made areas supervised by government and nongovernment agencies in order to make the best use of their aesthetic, functional, and economic potential. More importantly, the professionals must always be aware that the resources are for the optimum use of people.

PROFESSIONAL GOALS

One of the distinct characteristics of a profession is a broad commitment by its members to certain fundamental values or objectives. The members of a profession are not expected to think alike at all times, but they are obligated to agree upon central purposes. Such an agreement is essential to providing unity and ensuring the survival of the profession.

Almost twenty-five hundred years ago, Socrates emphasized the importance of goals when he said, "If a man does not know to what port he is sailing, no wind is favorable." The challenge of having clear direction has real pertinence to the individual leader because his or her worth will be no greater than the values sought. Further, leaders with unsound values tend not only to be worthless but have the potential for being dangerous to society.

Fortunately, in 1964 the Commission on Goals for American Recreation was established by the American Association for Health, Physical Education, and Recreation. The commission, consisting of outstanding leaders from throughout the nation, prepared statements that have had significant impact. Any person considering the recreation profession ought to become familiar with these goals in addition to giving serious thought to what he or she wants to achieve individually. Following are condensed descriptions of the goals established by the commission.

Personal Fulfillment. Since the American democratic ideal is rooted in a conviction of superior importance of the individual, it follows that the individual's welfare and personal development should be a primary goal of public and private programs that are geared toward service. In accord with this concept, the paramount purpose of recreational activities is to enrich the lives of people by contributing to their fulfillment as individuals while at the same time helping them to fit more comfortably into the social structure.

It is natural for people to be motivated by the basic need for adequacy and self-enrichment. Nobody wants to be a nobody. Individuals want to see themselves as accepted, able, and successful. The extent to which this need is met is a measure of personal fulfillment while the lack of fulfillment contributes toward frustration and often maladjustment.

One of the foremost challenges to people in the recreation profession is to provide experiences through which the individual may enjoy success in search for self-esteem. It is the task of a leader to assist participants in the development of skills and appreciations that enrich them and result in true satisfaction.

Democratic Human Relations. There are three important reasons why recreation involvement should contribute to the qualities of the good citizen in a democracy:

- A recreation agency in the United States is a social institution in a democratic nation. Therefore, the leaders are under obligation to seek social, moral, and ethical values that will preserve and strengthen the democracy.
- Exclusive emphasis on goals focused primarily on the individual may result in the creation of selfishness and noncooperation. Recreation agencies, along with other institutions in

society, have the responsibility to help develop those characteristics of good citizenship that are essential in a democracy.
• Whether they understand or desire it, recreation leaders are
  inescapably involved in the conduct of activities whose out-
  comes go far beyond fun, relaxation, and immediate fulfillment. Experiences in recreation, like other experiences in life,
  influence one's personality in many respects.

Leisure Skills and Interests. It is no coincidence that the words
"skills" and "interests" appear together often, for skill is the foundation upon which interest is built, and interest leads to the further
development of skill. In their leisure time people do, if opportunities
are available, what they like to do and often like to do what they do
well. A high degree of skill in a wholesome activity is the best single
guarantee of interest. Not many people, for example, are clamoring
to demonstrate their ineptness in tennis, golf, art, music, ballroom
dance, or swimming. There is plenty of evidence to support the
claim that people repeat those experiences that are satisfying and
avoid those that are dissatisfying. Therefore, the development of
skills and interests in wholesome activities is fundamental to the
well-rounded development of the individual and to the good life.

Several research studies support the claim that people use their
leisure time in the skills and interests developed early in life.
There also is evidence that what people like at age twenty-five
they like better with increased age, and what they dislike at age
twenty-five they dislike more as age advances. Recreation leaders
have a strong obligation to be teachers of interests and skills at a
level of excellence to both youth and adults, cultivating in them
tastes for beauty in art, music, dance, and literature, and helping
them to achieve excellence in sports and games and to enjoy the
beauty of nature while maintaining a highly livable environment.

Health and Fitness. In early history most people had no choice
between the sedentary and active life; the necessities of survival
forced them to be active. Modern men and women, however, do

have choices, and urbanization and technology have reduced opportunities for vigorous exercise. Today 98 percent of the work done in the United States is done by machines, 1 percent by animals, and 1 percent by people. Automation is the servant of the sedentary life.

Prior to our mass-motorized transportation system, people walked to most places. Today we ride automobiles with power brakes, power steering, power windows, and power seats. Even on the golf course motorized carts have become a substitute for human energy. Elevators carry us upstairs, electric eyes open doors for us, we sit before the television screen an average of sixteen hours per week. We engage in sports merely as spectators, and our most popular outdoor recreation is automobile riding for pleasure. Several degenerative diseases and general lack of efficiency have greatly accelerated with our modern sedentary living patterns.

In connection with fitness and health, the challenge and the opportunity in the field of recreation is apparent. If our work does not supply us with the activity we need for good health and fitness, then this must be accomplished during leisure hours.

Another interesting aspect of active living is the contribution it can make toward mental health and emotional stability. Participation in pleasurable pursuits is important to the release of tension and mental stress.

Creative Expression and Aesthetic Appreciation. In order to give depth and richness to life, emphasis needs to be given to creative experiences and aesthetics. Industrial and technological advances have created an emphasis on practicality, which has generally detracted from creative and aesthetic expression. There seems to be a lack of serenity in which creative thought and talent may be fostered. One of the important purposes of recreation is to stimulate and guide creativity that might otherwise never surface. Pursuits that relate to aesthetic values have great potential for giving zest to life, and we need well-qualified leaders who are creative themselves and who have the ability to stimulate others and draw out of them their innate creative expression.

Environment for Living in a Leisure Society. The environment in which each of us recreates, either alone or with others, has a great influence on the quality of the recreation experience. One of the tragedies of our time is the degradation and destruction of natural resources that heretofore sustained both body and soul. We have become too free in the use of tools and machines for converting natural products to utilitarian ends, serving only today's needs. This has contributed to an artificial and culturally sterile environment that doesn't serve the long-term needs of the people well. In the future we will have to guard with increased vigor against this destructive trend.

The recreational environment in the cities and suburbs is equally as important as the great outdoors, and the problem of maintaining it at a high level is even more difficult. About 75 percent of the American population now lives in urban and suburban areas, and the trend both in numbers and percentages is still rising. It is predicted by the Bureau of Census that in the near future 80 percent of Americans will be urban dwellers. Only with expert planning and leadership will highly livable city environments be developed and maintained. Sustaining such environments will be one of the great challenges of the future, particularly for recreation planners and administrators.

CHAPTER 5

EDUCATIONAL TRAINING

Our surroundings can enrich or impoverish our lives.
Thus conserving and improving our environment can add
immeasurably to private and public happiness.

Hubert H. Humphrey

The field of recreation has broadened immensely over the past
decade. Positions in the field run the spectrum and include administration, supervisory, and other leadership positions. Employment is
found in public, private, and volunteer settings. Professionals in this
field equip themselves with education and professional experiences.

Generally speaking, the professional in this field must be a promoter, a planner, an organizer, a teacher, and a motivator. If he or
she is to serve a worthwhile purpose, his or her efforts must be
based on a sound sense of values that will cause leadership to
actually benefit people. No wonder those who work in this interesting field find it challenging, exciting, and rewarding.

A major goal among those in the park and recreation field is the
development of a clear and favorable public image—an image of
professional competency and dedicated service. In fact, in the past
there has been a serious lack of public knowledge about the scope
and opportunities in leisure time occupations, and particularly
about the recreation profession. However, because of the increased
importance of leisure time occupations in recent years and
because of the strong present trend in that direction, this lack of

understanding is being overcome rapidly. There is an increased awareness in communities across the nation of the need for competent and well-prepared recreational leaders.

EARLY CAREER EXPLORATION

Most leisure time occupations involve working effectively with people. Further, these occupations usually involve a knowledge and intense interest in a variety of activities. You can begin preparing for a leisure time career while still in high school. Communications, art, physical education, and vocational arts provide a valuable background. Other courses that furnish leadership experiences, improve your ability to speak effectively, and teach you how to understand people also are beneficial.

Participation in extracurricular activities is strongly recommended. Sports, dramatics, music, debate, editing of school publications, and participation in hobby groups help to develop skills, special interests, and ability to work with others.

The U.S. Office of Education has designed a bold program of career education in which the various career fields that students in secondary schools ought to consider have been grouped into fifteen clusters. One of the clusters is identified as leisure careers. Robert M. Worthington, associate commissioner of the U.S. Office of Education made the following statement about leisure careers.

> Of the fifteen clusters forming this new design, the leisure careers are among the most promising. Americans seeking leisure time experiences will create millions of new jobs in the near future. Many of these jobs will be innovative and imaginative. Their environments will range from the natural wilderness to electronic playgrounds, and perhaps even more important, central to the leisure careers is per-

sonal interaction—a facet the majority of today's youth demand in a job.

This statement indicates a trend in leisure career employment.

The U.S. Office of Education career development program, which encompasses four important phases, is one that can be initiated and designed by school administrators and teachers, or it can be done individually by students. The purpose of the career development approach is to help you determine more intelligently where your interests lie and what abilities you have.

- *Phase 1—Career Awareness.* This phase should start early in a student's education and does not necessarily have an ending point. It includes recognition of the personal and social significance of work, fosters an awareness of the many occupations that one might consider, and builds aspirations to contribute and to succeed.

- *Phase 2—Career Exploration.* The purpose of this phase is to provide experiences that will assist students in evaluating their interests, abilities, values, and deeds as they relate to occupational roles, and also to cause basic subject matter to be more meaningful and relevant through focusing subject matter around a clearly developed theme.

- *Phase 3—Career Orientation.* The purpose of this phase is to provide in-depth training in one of the occupational clusters while still leaving open the option to move to a different occupational field, and also to focus subject matter even more directly to a career development theme. This phase also should include guidance and counseling relative to preparing for a particular field.

- *Phase 4—Skill Development.* The purpose of this phase is to provide the student with specific intellectual and performance skills in a selected occupational cluster or specific occupational field in order to better prepare him or her for job entry and/or continuing education. Further, the purpose is to motivate the student to become committed to the development of excellence of the self and of the chosen occupational field.

This four-phase approach will make you more aware of the opportunities and requirements of each career field. For a basic awareness of the leisure career field, you need answers to these questions: What is leisure? What is the leisure career field? What are the opportunities for employment and advancement? What is the future occupational outlook in this field? What are the basic requirements for employment? and What approach should you take to prepare for the particular occupational specialty of your choice?

STATUS OF PROFESSIONAL PREPARATION

Recreation and park curricula currently exist in more than 180 two-year colleges and almost 310 four-year colleges. There has been a phenomenal increase in the number of curricula since the end of World War II, when there were approximately a dozen. By 1950, there were 38 college curricula. In 1960, there were 63. In 1970, 227 institutions reported curricula in this field, and in 1982 the number totaled 354. These numbers have continued to grow and are expected to rise as recreation and leisure careers gain acceptance.

The curriculum is housed in a variety of divisions and departments including health, physical education, and recreation; education; forestry; natural resources; arts and sciences; and business and public relations.

The numbers of doctoral and master's degree programs have also increased over the past decade.

PROFESSIONAL PREPARATION PROGRAMS

In the recent past there has been a serious shortage of well-prepared professional recreation personnel. As a result, there has been a sharp increase during the last twenty years in the number of colleges and universities offering professional preparation programs in this field. This has greatly increased the number of college graduates in the field, and this trend will continue in the near future.

It is important to recognize that the college and university recreation departments are not the only programs involved in supplying this professional field. A portion of the leaders in the leisure industries have degrees in liberal arts, physical education, forestry, sociology, business, landscape architecture, industrial arts, and the fine arts.

Resource-oriented recreation curricula generally are housed in schools of forestry or natural resources, while recreational education and administration curricula are included predominately in schools of health, physical education, and recreation.

Fieldwork is another important part of a student's formal training in parks and recreation. Practically all of the institutions include some on-the-job experience for credit. The majority offer fieldwork opportunities in municipal recreation programs, and about half provide opportunities with hospitals and therapeutic agencies. A few have arrangements for fieldwork with natural resource management agencies, school camps, and volunteer agencies, as well as with industrial organizations.

Currently recreation and leisure curricula are found across the United States and Canada in the former associate, bachelor's, master's, and doctorate programs. Following is a brief definition of each degree program and then a list of schools in the United States and Canada offering recreation and leisure related curricula. The list contains the school name, program/department name, contact address, and degree(s) offered (not all information available for all schools).

ASSOCIATE DEGREE PROGRAMS

Today more than 180 two-year colleges offer curricula in the recreation and park field. The rapid increase in two-year associate degree programs can be attributed to two major factors: expansion of the number of two-year colleges, and the demand for direct leaders and program technicians who need less than a four-year college degree. The role of two-year associate degree programs in recreation is to prepare students for face-to-face leadership positions or technician jobs. These programs prepare students for early entry into the field and/or transfer to four-year programs to continue education toward a bachelor's degree. The kinds of jobs available to people with associate degrees include director of playground activities, swimming pool manager or swimming instructor, leader of athletic activities, park ranger (in some areas), and park maintenance supervisor.

BACHELOR DEGREE PROGRAMS

Typically in bachelor degree programs about 50 percent of the course work is in general education including humanities, language arts, physical and social sciences, English and writing skills. The remaining 50 percent is in a specialized field and related electives. In addition to course work in the specialty, a student majoring in recreation ordinarily has extensive on-the-job-training under the combined supervision of a specialist in the field and a faculty supervisor. As stated earlier, nearly 200 colleges and universities in the United States offer bachelor's degrees in the recreation and park field.

GRADUATE PREPARATION

Often the administrators of the large and more complex recreation and park programs are required to hold master's degrees, and college teachers and research specialists almost always must earn at least a master's degree and, preferably, a doctorate. The areas that ordinarily receive emphasis at the graduate level include Philosophy and Principles Related to Recreation and Leisure; Adminstrative Philosophy and Procedures; Research and Evaluation Techniques; Advanced Approaches to Personal Management; Public Relations. Sometimes more specialized areas are pursued at the graduate levels, such as Therapeutic Recreation or Management of Outdoor Recreation Resources or Park Administration.

SCHOLARSHIPS AND INTERNSHIPS

A national internship program is provided through the National Recreation and Park Association (NRPA). It provides special advanced training for a number of college graduates showing outstanding potential for administrative careers in the field. Stipends varying from $8,000 to $10,000 per year are awarded by agencies selected to administer these internships. The host agency also provides a broad based and diversified experience designed to move the intern quickly into a responsible administrative position. These agencies located throughout the country are representative of all facets of the park, recreation, and conservation field. Information about how to apply may be obtained from the NRPA.

The scholarship office of every college or university will furnish information upon request about scholarships offered by the particular institution. In some cases the specific department where the recreation curriculum is administered has limited financial aid available for selected students.

COLLEGES AND UNIVERSITIES
THAT OFFER CURRICULA RELATED
TO RECREATION AND LEISURE*

United States

Alabama

Alabama State University
   Health, Physical Education and
      Recreation
   P.O. Box 271
   Montgomery, AL 36101
   B.A.

Auburn University
   Recreation Admin. Program
      Area
   2050 Memorial Coliseum
   Auburn, AL 36849
   B.A.

Community College of the Air
      Force
   Associates

Jefferson State Community
      College
   Dept. of Health, Physical
      Education, and Recreation
   2601 Carson Road
   Birmingham, AL 35215
   A.A.S.

Stillman College
   Recreation Program
   P.O. Box 1430
   Tuscaloosa, AL 35401
   B.A.

University of South Alabama
   Leisure Studies
   307 University Boulevard
   Mobile, AL 36688
   B.S. in Leisure Studies
   M.S. in Recreation
      Admin.
   M.S. in Therapeutic Recreation

Arizona

Arizona State University
   Dept. of Recreation Mgmt. and
      Tourism
   P.O. Box 874905
   Tempe, AZ 85287-7291
   B.S. and M.S. in Recreation

*College/university information from the 1998/1999 *Curriculum Catalog,*
published by the Society of Park and Recreation Educators, a branch of the
National Recreation and Park Association, Ashburn, Virginia, copyright
1997.

And the National Recreation and Park Association 1999 computer listing
of professional preparation programs in recreation, parks, and related
areas.

Arizona State University West
  Dept. of Recreation and
    Tourism Mgmt.
  4701 West Thunderbird Road
  P.O. Box 37100
  Phoenix, AZ 85069-7100
  B.S.

Central Arizona College
  Associates

Glendale Community College
  Associates

Northern Arizona University
  Parks and Recreation Mgmt.
    Program
  Box 15018
  Flagstaff, AZ 86011-5018
  B.A.

Northland Pioneer College
  Associates

Pima Community College
  Tucson, AZ 85709
  Associates

University of Arizona
  Wildlife, Fish, Recreational
    Resources Division
  School of Renewable Natural
    Resources
  Tucson, AZ 85721
  B.A., M.A., Ph.D., Dir.

Arkansas

Arkansas Tech University
  Parks, Recreation, and
    Hospitality Admin.
  Williamson 106
  Russellville, AR 72801
  B.A.

Central Arkansas University
  B.A.

Henderson State University
  Recreation Division, HPER
  HSU Box 7552
  Arkadelphia, AR 71999-0001
  B.A.

Southern Arkansas University
  Dept. of Health, Kinesiology,
    and Recreation
  SAU Bos 1329
  Magnolia, AR 71753
  B.A.

Southern Baptist College
  Walnut Ridge, AR
  Associates

University of Arkansas,
    Fayetteville
  Dept. of Health Science,
    Kinesiology, Recreation, and
    Dance
  Fayetteville, AR 72701
  B.S., M.A.T., M.Ed., M.S.,
    Ed.D., Ph.D.

University of Arkansas, Pine Bluff
  Dept. of HPER
  North University Avenue
  Pine Bluff, AR 71601
  B.A., M.A., Doctorate

California

American River College
  Sacramento, CA 95841
  Associates

Antelope Valley College
  Lancaster, CA 93534
  Associates

Bakersfield College
Associates

Cal Poly, Pomona
Park and Recreation Program
Pomona, CA
B.A.

California Polytechnic State
University–San Luis Obispo
Natural Resources Mgmt. Dept.
San Luis Obispo, CA 93407
B.S.

California State University, Carson
B.A.

California State University, Chico
Dept. of Recreation and Parks
Mgmt.
Tehama 101
Chico, CA 95929-0560

California State University,
Dominguez Hills
Recreation and Leisure Studies,
PERD
1000 E. Victoria Street
Carson, CA 90747
B.S. and M.A. in Recreation
Admin.

California State University, Fresno
Recreation Admin. and Leisure
Studies Program
5310 N. Campus Drive M/S
#103
Fresno, CA 93740-8019
B.S.

California State University,
Hayward
Dept. of Recreation and
Community Services
Hayward, CA 94541
B.S.

California State University, Long
Beach
Dept. of Recreation and
Leisure Studies
1250 Bellflower Boulevard
Long Beach, CA 90840-4903
B.S. in Recreation
M.S. in Recreation Admin.

California State University,
Northridge
Dept. of Leisure Studies and
Recreation
18111 Nordhoff Street
Northridge, CA 91330-8269
B.S. in Recreation
B.S. in Recreation, Therapeutic
Recreation Option
M.S. in Recreation Admin.

California State University,
Sacramento
Dept. of Recreation and
Leisure Studies
6000 J Street
Sacramento, CA 95819-6110
B.S., Minor, Certificate, M.S.

Cerritos College
Associates

Chabot College
Hayward, CA 94545
Associates

Chaffey College
Associates

College of Marin
Associates

College of the Canyons
Valencia, CA 95501
Associates

College of the Desert
Associates

College of the Redwoods
Associates

Contra Costa College
Associates

Cypress College
Associates

Feather River College
Quincy, CA 95971
Associates

Foothill College
Associates

Fresno City College
Fresno City, CA 93741
Associates

Humboldt State University
Arcata, CA 95521
B.A.

Pepperdine University, Seaver
College
Malibu, CA 90265
B.A.

San Diego State University
Dept. of Recreation, Parks, and
Tourism
San Diego, CA 92182-4531
B.S. in Recreation Admin. with
emphasis in: Recreation
Therapy, Recreation
Systems Mgmt., and Outdoor
Recreation

San Francisco State University
Dept. of Recreation and
Leisure Studies
San Francisco, CA 94132
B.A., B.S., M.S.

San Jose State University
Dept. of Recreation and
Leisure Studies
One Washington Square
San Jose, California 95192-
0060
B.S. and M.S.

University of California, Davis
Davis, CA 95616
B.A.

University of California, Los
Angeles
B.A., M.A., Ph.D.

University of LaVerne
B.A.

University of Southern California
B.A.

University of the Pacific
B.A.

Ventura College
B.A., M.A.

Whittier College
Dept. of Recreation and
Physical Education
13426 E. Philadelphia
Whittier, CA 90608

Colorado

Adams State College
HPER Dept.
Plachy Hall
Alamoca, CO 81102
B.A., M.A.

Colorado Mountain College
Outdoor Recreation Leadership
Program
901 South Highway 24
Leadville, CO 80461
A.G.S. (Associate in Graduate
Studies)

Colorado State University
Dept. of Natural Resource
Recreation and Tourism
Fort Collins, CO 80523
B.S., M.S., Ph.D. of Philosophy

Mesa College
Dept. of Physical Education,
Recreation, and Leisure
Saunders Center, P.O. Box 2647
Grand Junction, CO 81502
B.A.

Metropolitan State College of
Denver
Dept. of Human Performance,
Sport and Leisure Studies
P.O. Box 173362
Campus Box 25
Denver, CO 80217-3362
B.A. in Leisure Studies

University of Colorado, Boulder
Tourism and Recreation
Campus Box 420
Boulder, CO 80309
B.A., M.A.

University of Northern Colorado
Recreation Program
Gunter 1250
Greeley, CO 80639
B.S.

University of Southern Colorado
Human Performance and
Leisure Studies
Massari Gym
Pueblo, CO 81001-4901
B.A.

Western State College of Colorado
Kinesiology and Recreation
Dept.
Paul Wright Gym
Gunnison, CO 81231
B.A.

Connecticut

Eastern Connecticut State
University
B.A.

Mitchell College
Dept. of Physical Education,
Recreation, and Fitness
437 Pequot Avenue
New London, CT 06320
A.S. in Therapeutic Recreation

Southern Connecticut State
University
Dept. of Recreation and
Leisure Studies
Building TE-5
New Haven, CT 06515
B.A., M.A.

The University of Connecticut
Dept. of Sport Leisure and
Exercise Sciences
Grampel Pavilion
2095 Hillside Road
Storrs, CT 06269-1110
B.S., M.A., 6th Year Diploma,
and Ph.D.

Delaware

Delaware State University
HPER Dept.
1200 N. Dupont Highway
Dover, DE
B.A.

University of Delaware
  Recreation Dept.
  Carpenter Sports Building
  Newark, DE 19716

District of Columbia

Gallaudet University
  Recreation and Leisure Studies
    Program
  Field House
  Washington, DC 20002-3695
  B.S.

George Washington University
  Washington, DC
  B.A.

Howard University
  Washington, DC 20059
  B.A., M.A.

University of the District of
    Columbia
  B.A., M.A.

Florida

Eckerd College
  Human Resources/Leisure
    Services
  P.O. Box 12560
  St. Petersburg, FL 33733
  B.A.

Florida A&M University
  Tallahassee, FL

Florida International University
  Park and Recreation Mgmt.
  Dept. of HPERA/GPA 242
  Miami, FL 33199
  B.A., M.A.

Florida State University
  Program in Recreation and
    Leisure Services Admin.
  215 Stone Building
  Tallahassee, FL 32306-3001
  B.S., M.S.

North Florida University
  HPER Dept.
  Box 16761
  Jacksonville, FL 32216
  B.A., M.A.

University of Florida
  Dept. of Recreation, Parks, and
    Tourism
  P.O. Box 118208
  Gainesville, FL 32611-8208
  B.S., M.S., Ph.D.

University of Central Florida
  Dept. of Hospitality
  Orlando, FL 32816-3245
  B.A.

University of Miami
  Physical Therapy, Exercise
    Science, Sport Studies
  Coral Gables, FL 33124
  B.A., M.A.

University of West Florida
  HLS Dept.
  Pensacola, FL 32514
  B.A., M.A.

Warner Southern College
  Lake Wales, FL

Georgia

Columbus College
  Physical Education and Leisure
    Mgmt.
  Algonquin Drive
  Columbus, GA 31933
  B.A.

Columbus State University
  Recreation and Park Admin.
    Program, PELM
  4225 University Avenue
  Columbus, GA 31907-5645
  Associates, B.A.

Georgia Southern University
  Dept. of Recreation and Sport
    Mgmt.
  P.O. Box 8077
  Statesboro, GA 30460-8077
  B.S. in Recreation
  B.S. in Sport Mgmt.
  M.A. Recreation Admin.
  M.S. Sport Mgmt.

Georgia State University
  Recreation and Leisure Studies
  125 Decatur Street
  Atlanta, GA 30303
  B.A., M.A.

Morris Brown College
  Atlanta, GA

North Georgia College
  Recreation Curriculum, HPER
  Dahlonega, GA 30597
  B.A.

Shorter College
  Recreation Mgmt. Program
  Rome, GA 30161
  B.A.

Thomas College
  Environmental Recreation
    Mgmt.
  1501 Millpond Road
  Thomasville, GA 31792
  B.A.

University of Georgia
  Dept. of Recreation and
    Leisure Studies
  300 River Road
  Ramsey Center
  Athens, GA 30602-3655
  B.S., M.Ed., M.A., Ed.D.

West Georgia College
  Dept. of Physical Education and
    Recreation
  Carrollton, GA 30118
  B.A.

Hawaii

University of Hawaii
  Recreation and Leisure Science
    Program
  1337 Lower Campus Road
  Honolulu, HI 96822
  B.A.

Idaho

Northwest Nazarene College
  B.A.

University of Idaho
  Dept. of Recreation
  Memorial Gym Building
  Moscow, ID 83844-2429
  B.S. in Recreation
  M.S. in Sport and Recreation
    Mgmt.

University of Idaho
Dept. of Resource Recreation
and Tourism
Sixth and Line Streets
Moscow, ID 83844-1139
B.S., M.S., Ph.D.

Illinois

Aurora University
Recreation Admin. Dept.
347 S. Gladstone Avenue
Aurora, IL 60506
B.S., M.S.

Chicago State University
HPER Dept.
Jacoby Dickens Center 216
Chicago, IL 60628-1598
B.A., M.A.

Eastern Illinois University
Dept. of Leisure Studies
McAfee Building
Charleston, IL 61920
B.S.

Elmhurst College
Elmhurst, IL 60126
B.A.

Illinois State University
Recreation and Park Admin.
Program
101 McCormick Hall
Normal, IL 61790-5121
B.S. Recreation and Park
Admin.
M.S. Health, Physical
Education, and Recreation

Kennedy-King College
Chicago, IL 60621
B.A.

McKendree College
Lebanon, IL 62254
B.A.

Northeastern Illinois University
Chicago, IL 60625
B.A.

Southern Illinois University at
Carbondale
Dept. of Health Education and
Recreation
Pulliam Hall 307
Mailcode 4632
Carbondale, IL 62901-4632
B.S. in Education (Recreation)
M.S. in Education (Recreation)

University of Illinois at Urbana-
Champaign
Dept. of Leisure Studies
104 Huff Hall
1206 S. Fourth Street
Champaign, IL 61820
B.S. in Leisure Studies
M.S. in Leisure Studies
Ph.D. with specialization in
Leisure Studies

University of St. Francis
Dept. of Recreation Admin.
Tower Hall
Joliet, IL 60435
B.A.

Western Illinois University
Dept. of Recreation, Park, and
Tourism Admin.
400 Currens Hall
Macomb, IL 61455
B.S., M.Ed.

Indiana

Anderson College
Anderson, IN
B.A.

Ball State University
Muncie, IN 47306
B.A., M.A.

Huntington College
Huntington, IN 46570
B.A.

Indiana Institute of Technology
B.A.

Indiana State University
Dept. of Recreation and Sport
Mgmt.
HHP Building
Room B-64
Terre Haute, IN 47809
B.S. in Recreation and Sport
Mgmt.
M.S. in Recreation and Sport
Mgmt.

Indiana State University,
Evansville
Evansville, IN
B.A.

Indiana University
Dept. of Recreation and Park
Admin.
Bloomington, IN 47405
B.S., M.S., Re.Dir., Re.D.,
Ph.D.

Purdue University
PEHRS Dept.
Lambert Gym
West Lafayette, IN 47907
B.A., M.A., Ph.D.

Taylor University
HPER Dept.
500 W. Read Avenue
Upland, IN 46989-1001
B.A.

Vincennes University
Recreation and Leisure Studies
Dept.
Physical Education Complex
Vincennes, IN 47591
B.A.

Iowa

Central College
B.A.

Drake University
Des Moines, IA 50311
B.A., M.A.

Graceland College
Lamoni, IA 50140
B.A.

Iowa State University
Ames, IA 50011
B.A.

Morningside College
B.A.

Northwestern College
Orange City, IA
B.A.

The University of Iowa
Dept. of Sport, Health, Leisure,
and Physical Studies
E102 Field House
Iowa City, IA 52242
B.S. and M.A. in Sport, Health,
Leisure, and Physical Studies

University of Northern Iowa
Leisure Services Division
Cedar Falls, IA 50614-0161
B.A. in Leisure Services, with
options in Programming and
Therapeutic Recreation
M.A. in Leisure Services-
Youth/Human Service
Agency Admin.

Upper Iowa University
B.A.

Wartburg College
Waverly, IA 50677
B.A.

Kansas

Emporia State University
Emporia, KS 66801
B.A.

Kansas State University
Dept. of Horticulture, Forestry,
and Recreation Resources
Manhattan, KS 66506-5506
B.S.

Mid-America Nazarene College
Olathe, KS 66061
B.A.

Pittsburg State University
HPER Dept.
243 Weed
Pittsburg, KS 66762-7557
B.A., M.A.

University of Kansas
Lawrence, KS 66045
B.A., M.A.

Wichita State University
Wichita, KS 67217
B.A.

Kentucky

Asbury College
Dept. of Recreation
Lexington Avenue
Wilmore, KY 40390
B.A.

Cumberland College
Dept. of Recreation
Cumberland College Station
Williamsburg, KY 40769
B.A.

Eastern Kentucky University
Dept. of Recreation and Park
Admin.
Richmond, KY 40475
B.S. in Recreation and Park
Admin.
M.S. in Recreation and Park
Admin.

Georgetown College
Recreation Program
Georgetown, KY 40324
B.A.

Morehead State University
Physical Education and
Recreation
Morehead, KY 40351
B.A.

Murray State University
HPER Dept.
P.O. Box 9
Murray, KY
B.A., M.A.

University of Kentucky
Lexington, KY
B.A., M.A.

University of Louisville
Physical Education and
Recreation
Belknap Campus
Louisville, KY 40208
B.A.

Western Kentucky University
Dept. of Physical Education and
Recreation
1 Big Red Way
Bowling Green, KY 42101-
3576
B.S., M.S.

Louisiana

Grambling State University
Dept. of Health, Physical
Education, and Recreation
Grambling, LA 71245
B.S. in Leisure Studies with
emphasis in: Therapeutic
Recreation and Recreation
Program Service Delivery

Southern A&M University
Dept. of Curriculum and
Instruction
P.O. Box 9752
Baton Rouge, LA 70813
B.A., M.A.

Southern University, New Orleans
1401 Foucher Street
New Orleans, LA 70115
B.A.

University of Southwestern
Louisiana
Health and Physical Education
Dept.
Lafayette, LA 70506
B.A.

Maine

Unity College
Unity, ME 04988
B.A.

University of Maine, Machias
Program in Recreation Mgmt.
9 O'Brian Avenue
Machias, ME 04654
Associates, B.A.

University of Maine at Presque
Isle
Dept. of Recreation and
Leisure Services
181 Main Street
Normal Hall
Presque Isle, ME 04769
B.S. in Recreation/Leisure
Services
B.S. in Recreation/Leisure
Services, Park Law
Enforcement emphasis
Minor in Recreation/Leisure
Services
Associate of Arts in Recreation/
Leisure Services

University of New England
Biddeford, ME

University of Southern Maine
Dept. of Recreation and
Leisure Studies
96 Falmouth Street
P.O. Box 9300
Portland, ME 04104-9300

Maryland

Coppin State
B.A.

Frostburg State University
Recreation Program
PE Building
Frostburg, MD 21532
B.S., M.S.

University of Baltimore
Baltimore, MD 21201
B.A., M.A.

University of Maryland
College Park, MD 20742
M.A., Ph.D.

Massachusetts

Boston University
Leisure Studies Program
704 Commonwealth Avenue
Boston, MA 02215

Bridgewater State College
B.A.

Gordon College
Park and Recreation Program
255 Grapevine Road
Wenham, MA 01984
B.A.

Northeastern University
Boston, MA 02115
B.A., M.A.

Springfield College
Dept. of Recreation and
Leisure Services
B.S. degrees in: Therapeutic
Recreation, Recreation
Mgmt., and Outdoor
Recreation Mgmt. M.ED.,
M.S. degrees in: Therapeutic
Recreation Mgmt.,
Recreation Mgmt., and
Outdoor Recreation Mgmt.

University of Massachusetts,
Amherst
Amherst, MA 01003
Associates, B.A.

Michigan

Calvin College
Grand Rapids, MI 49506
B.A.

Central Michigan University
Dept. of Recreation, Parks, and
Leisure Services Admin.
Finch Building 115
Mt. Pleasant, MI 48859
B.A., B.A.A., B.S., M.A., M.S.

Eastern Michigan University
Recreation Division, HPERD
235 Warner
Ypsilanti, MI 48197
B.A.

Ferris State University
Dept. Leisure Studies and
Wellness
SW Commons 202
901 S. State Street
Big Rapids, MI 49307-2295
B.A.

Grand Valley State University
Therapeutic Recreation
Program
327 Padnos
Allendale, MI 49401
B.S. in Therapeutic Recreation

Lake Superior State University
Recreation Studies and Exercise
Science
Norris Center
Sault Ste. Marie, MI 49783
B.A.

Michigan State University
Dept. of Park, Recreation, and
Tourism Resources
Room 131 Natural Resources
Building
East Lansing, MI 48824-1222
B.S., M.S., Ph.D.

Northern Michigan University
Marquette, MI
B.A., M.A.

Northwestern Michigan University
Traverse City, MI 49684
B.A.

University of Michigan
Ann Arbor, MI 48109
B.A., M.A., Ph.D.

Wayne State University
Recreation and Park Services
259 Matthaei Building
Detroit, MI 48202

Western Michigan University
Dept. of Health, Physical
Education, and Recreation
Student Recreation Center
Kalamazoo, MI 49008-3871
B.S. Recreation Major and
Minor (Nonteaching)

Minnesota

Bemidji State University
HPER Dept.
Bemidji, MN 56601
B.A.

Mankato State University
Dept. of Recreation, Parks, and
Leisure Services
213 Highland North
Mankato, MN 46002-8400
B.S. in Recreation, Parks, and
Leisure Services
M.S. in Multidisciplinary
Recreation

St. Cloud University
Recreation Admin., Dept.
HPERSS
Halenbeck Hall
St. Cloud, MN 56301-4498
B.A.

University of Minnesota
  Division of Recreation, Park,
    and Leisure Studies
  224 Cooke Hall
  1900 University Avenue S. E.
  Minneapolis, MN 55455
  B.S., M.Ed., M.A. in
    Recreation, Park, and Leisure
    Studies
  Ph.D. in Education and Human
    Development (emphasis in
    Recreation, Park, and Leisure
    Studies)

University of Minnesota, Duluth
  HPER Dept.
  Sport and Health Center 110
  Duluth, MN 55812
  B.A.

University of Minnesota, St. Paul
  Recreational Resource Mgmt.
  1530 N. Cleveland Avenue
  St. Paul, MN 55108
  B.A., M.A., Ph.D.

Winona State University
  Recreation and Leisure Studies
  126 Memorial Hall
  Winona, MN 55987
  B.A., M.A.

Mississippi

Alcorn State University
  HPER Dept.
  P.O. Box 510
  Lorman, MS 39096
  B.A.

Jackson State University
  HPER Dept.
  1400 J. P. Lynch Street
  Jackson, MS 39217
  B.A.

University of Mississippi
  Dept. of Exercise Science and
    Leisure Mgmt.
  Turner Center
  University, MS 38677
  B.A., M.A., and Ph.D. in
    Exercise Science and Leisure
    Mgmt.

University of Southern Mississippi
  School of Human Performance
    and Recreation
  Box 5142
  Hattiesburg, MS 39406-5142
  B.S., M.S.

Missouri

Central Missouri State University
  Recreation and Tourism
  201 Lovinger Building
  Warrensburg, MO 64093
  B.A., M.A.

Evangel College
  Springfield, MO 65802
  B.A.

Missouri Western State College
  HPER Dept.
  4525 Downs Drive
  St. Joseph, MO 64507
  B.A.

Northeast Missouri State
    University
  Kirksville, MO 63501
  B.A.

Northwest Missouri State
University
Dept. of Health, Physical
Education, Recreation, and
Dance
205 Lamkin Activity Center
Maryville, MO 64468
B.S., M.S. Ed.

Southeast Missouri State
University
Dept. of Health and Leisure
One University Plaza
Cape Girardeau, MO 63701
B.S.

Southwest Baptist University
Bolivar, MO 65613
B.A.

Southwest Missouri State
University
Recreation and Leisure Studies
Springfield, MO 65804
B.S.

University of Missouri
Dept. of Parks, Recreation, and
Tourism
602 Clark Hall
Columbia, MO 65211
B.S., M.S.

Montana

Montana State University
HPER Dept.
Bozeman, MT 59717
B.A.

The University of Montana
Recreation Mgmt. Program
School of Forestry
Missoula, MT 59812
B.S., M.S., and Ph.D.

Nebraska

Chadron State College
Chadron, NE 69337
B.A.

College of St. Mary
HPER Dept.
Omaha, NE 68124
Associates, B.A.

Nebraska Wesleyan University
Lincoln, NE
B.A.

University of Nebraska, Kearney
Cushing Coliseum
Kearney, NE 68849
B.A.

University of Nebraska, Lincoln
Lincoln, NE 68504
B.A.

University of Nebraska, Omaha
Program in Recreation and
Leisure Studies
Omaha, NE 68182-0216
B.S., M.S., M.A.

Wayne State College
Wayne, NE 68787
B.A.

Nevada

Nevada University
Sport and Leisure Studies Dept.
B.A.

University of Nevada, Las Vegas
Dept. of Leisure Studies
4505 Maryland Parkway
Box 453035
Las Vegas, NV 89154-3035
B.S., M.S.

University of Nevada, Reno
  Health Ecology
  Reno, NV
  B.A.

New Hampshire

Franklin Pierce College
  Recreation Mgmt. Program
  P.O. Box 60
  Rindge, NH 03461
  B.A.

University of New Hampshire
  Dept. of Recreation Mgmt. and
    Policy
  108 Hewitt Hall
  Durham, NH 03824
  B.S., M.A.

New Jersey

Georgian Court College
  Institute for Tourism and
    Recreation Mgmt.
  Farley Business School
  Lakewood, NJ 08701
  B.S. in Business Administration
    with specialization in
    Tourism and Recreation
    Mgmt.

Jersey City State College
  2039 Kennedy Boulevard
  Jersey City, NJ 07305
  B.A.

Kean University
  Recreation Admin.
  Townsend 114
  Union, NJ 07083
  B.A.

Montclair State University
  Health Professions, PERLS
  Panzer Gym
  Upper Montclair, NJ 07043
  B.A.

Rutgers University
  Recreation and Leisure Studies
  College Avenue
  New Brunswick, NJ 08903
  B.A.

William Paterson College of New
    Jersey
  Wightman Gym 209
  Wayne, NJ 07470
  B.A.

New Mexico

New Mexico Highlands University
  Las Vegas, NM 87701
  Associates, B.A.

New Mexico State University, Las
    Cruces
  Hospitality and Tourism
    Services Program
  Box 30003
  Las Cruces, NM 88003

University of New Mexico
  Recreation Program, HPER
    Dept.
  Albuquerque, NM 87131
  B.A., M.A., Ph.D.

New York

Ithaca College
  Dept. of Therapeutic Recreation
    and Leisure Services
  11 Hill Center
  Ithaca, NY 14850
  B.S. in Leisure Services
  B.S. in Therapeutic Recreation

Lehman College of the City
    University of New York
  Leisure Sciences Program
  250 Bedford Park Boulevard
    West
  Bronx, NY 10468-1589
  B.S., M.S. Ed.

Medaille College
Buffalo, NY 14214
B.A., M.A.

Mercy College
Therapeutic Recreation
Program
555 Broadway
Dobbs Ferry, NY 10522
B.A.

New York University
Recreation and Leisure Studies,
Dept. Health Studies
35 W. 4th Street, Room 1200
New York, NY 10003
B.A.

Niagara University
Institute of Travel, Hotel, and
Restaurant Admin.
Niagara University, NY 14109
B.A.

St. Joseph's College
Recreation Dept.
Patchog, NY 11772
B.A., M.A.

State University of New York,
College at Brockport
Dept. of Recreation and
Leisure Studies
350 New Campus Drive
Brockport, NY 14420-2976
B.S., M.S.

State University of New York,
College at Cortland
Dept. of Recreation and
Leisure Studies
P.O. Box 2000
Cortland, NY 13045-0900
B.S., B.S.E., M.S., M.S.E.

State University of New York,
Syracuse
College of Environmental
Science and Forestry
One Forestry Drive
Syracuse, NY 13201-2778
B.A.

North Carolina

Appalachian State University
Leisure Studies Program
Boone, NC 28608
B.S. in Recreation Mgmt.

Belmont Abbey College
Recreational Studies
Wheeler Center
Belmont, NC 28012
B.A.

Catawba College
HPER Dept.
Salisbury, NC 28144
B.A.

East Carolina University
Dept. of Recreation and
Leisure Studies
Greenville, NC 27858-4353
B.S. in Recreation and Leisure
Studies

Elon College
Leisure/Sport Mgmt.
Campus Box 2233
Elon College, NC 27244
B.S.

Mars Hill College
Recreation Dept.
104 Chambers Gymnasium
Mars Hill, NC 28754
B.A.

Mount Olive College
Dept. of Recreation and
Leisure Studies
634 Henderson Street
Mount Olive, NC 28365

North Carolina Agricultural and
Technical University
Greensboro, NC 27412
B.A.

North Carolina Central University
Durham, NC 27707
B.A., M.A.

North Carolina State University
Dept. of Parks, Recreation, and
Tourism Mgmt.
Box 8004
4008 Biltmore Hall
Raleigh, NC 27695-8004
B.S., M.S., M.P.R.T.M., M. Nat.
Res.

University of North
Carolina–Chapel Hill
Curriculum in Leisure Studies
and Recreation Admin.
CB #3185 Evergreen House
Chapel Hill, NC 27599
B.A. Recreation Admin.
M.S. in Recreation Admin.
(M.S.R.A.)

University of North Carolina,
Greensboro
Dept. of Leisure Studies
420 J HHP Building
Greensboro, NC 27412
B.S., M.S.

University of North Carolina at
Wilmington
Dept. of Health, Physical
Education, and Recreation
601 S. College Road
Wilmington, NC 28403-3297
B.A. in Parks and Recreation
Mgmt.

Warren Wilson College
Outdoor Leadership Studies
Asheville, NC 28815-9000
B.A.

Western Carolina University
Parks and Recreation Mgmt.
Program
Reid Gym
Cullowhee, NC 28723
B.S.

Wingate College
Parks and Recreation Admin.
Program
Campus Box 3006/Burris
Building
Wingate, NC 28174
Associates, B.A.

Winston-Salem State University
Therapeutic Recreation
Program
Winston-Salem, NC 27110
B.A.

North Dakota

North Dakota State University,
Fargo
BSA Room 100
Fargo, ND 58105
B.A., M.A.

Minot State University–Bottineau
Parks and Recreation Program
105 Simrall Boulevard
Bottineau, ND 58318
A.A.S. in Parks and Recreation
Technology
A.S. in Park Mgmt.

University of North Dakota
Recreation and Leisure Services
Program
P.O. Box 8235
Grand Forks, ND 58202
B.S.

Ohio

Ashland University
Dept. of Sport Sciences
Physical Education Building
Ashland, OH 44805
B.S. Recreation Admin.
B.S. Therapeutic Recreation

Bowling Green State University
Sport Mgmt., Recreation, and
Tourism Division
203 Eppler North
Bowling Green, OH 43403
B.S. in Education
M.S. in Education

Central State University
Recreation Program, HPER
Dept.
Walker Gym
Wilberforce, OH 45294
B.A.

Kent State University
Leisure Studies
P.O. Box 5190
Kent, OH 44242
B.S., M.A.

Miami University of Ohio
Phillips Hall
Miami, OH 45056
B.A.

Ohio State University
Parks, Recreation, and Tourism
Admin.
210 Kottman Hall
Columbus, OH 43210
B.A., M.A.

Ohio University
School of Recreation and Sport
Sciences
Grover Center
Athens, OH 45701
B.S. in Recreation Studies
M.S. in Physical Education with
a concentration in Recreation

Shawnee State College
Portsmouth, OH 45662
B.A.

University of Cincinnati
B.A.

University of Findlay
Recreation Therapy Program
1000 North Main
Findlay, OH 45840
B.A.

University of Toledo
  Recreation and Leisure Studies
  252 Health Education Center
  2801 W. Bancroft Street
  Toledo, OH 43606
  B.Ed. with specialization in
    Resource Mgmt., Law
    Enforcement, Community
    Special Recreation,
    Community Recreation,
    Therapeutic Recreation
  M.Ed. with emphasis in
    Recreation Admin. or
    Therapeutic Recreation

Oklahoma

Eastern Oklahoma State College
  Park/Nursery Mgmt., Forest
    Technology
  Wilburton, OK 74578
  B.A.

Langston University
  P.O. Box 907
  Langston, OK 73050-0907
  B.A.

Oklahoma Panhandle State
  University
  B.A.

Oklahoma State University
  Leisure Studies
  Colvin Center
  Stillwater, OK 74078
  B.S. in Leisure Studies
  M.S. in HPEL, emphasis in
    Leisure Studies
  Doctor of Education in Applied
    Educational Studies
  Doctor of Philosophy in
    Environmental Science

Oral Roberts University
  B.A.

Southwestern Oklahoma State
  University
  100 Campus Drive
  Weatherford, OK
  B.A.

University of Central Oklahoma
  100 N. University Dr.
  Edmond, OK 73034-0170
  B.A.

University of Oklahoma
  HPER Dept.
  Admin. 1401 ASP
  Norman, OK 73019
  B.A., M.A.

University of Tulsa
  Tulsa, OK 74104
  B.A., M.A.

Oregon

Judson Baptist College
  The Dalles, OR 97058
  B.A.

Oregon State University
  Dept. of Forest Resources
  Peavy Hall 140
  Corvallis, OR 97331
  B.A., M.A.

University of Oregon
  RTMD–Academic Affairs
  Esslinger Hall 180
  Eugene, OR 97403
  B.A., M.A., Ph.D.

Pennsylvania

California University of
  Pennsylvania
  California, PA 15419
  B.A.

Cheyney State University
HPER Dept.
Cope Hall, Box 400
Cheyney, PA 19319
B.A.

East Stroudsburg University
Dept. of Recreation and
Leisure Services Mgmt.
East Stroudsburg, PA 18301
B.S. in Recreation and Leisure
Services Mgmt.

Gannon University
Erie, PA
Associates, B.A.

Lebanon Valley College
B.A.

Lincoln University
Dept. of Health, Physical
Education, and Recreation
Rivero Hall
Lincoln University, PA 19352
B.S. Recreation (option:
Therapeutic Recreation)

Lock Haven University
Recreation Dept.
22 Recreation/Honors House
Lock Haven, PA 17745
B.A.

Messiah College
HPER Dept.
Grantham, PA 17072
B.A.

Pennsylvania State University
Recreation and Park Mgmt.
Program
201 Mateer Building
University Park, PA 16802
B.S., M.S., M.Ed., and Ph.D.

Slippery Rock University
Dept. of Parks and Recreation/
Environmental Education
Slippery Rock, PA 16057
B.S., M.S., M.Ed.

Temple University
Dept. of Sport Mgmt. and
Leisure Studies
316 Seltzer Hall
Philadelphia, PA 19122
B.S. and M.Ed.

West Chester State College
West Chester, PA 19383
B.A.

Widener University
Chester, PA
B.A.

York College of Pennsylvania
Recreation and Leisure Admin.
Country Club Road
York, PA 17405-7199
B.S.

Rhode Island

Rhode Island College
Providence, RI 02908
B.A.

South Carolina

Benedict College
Recreation Dept.
Harden and Blanding Streets
Columbia, SC 29204
B.A.

Claflin College
Dept. of Health and Physical
Education
College Avenue
Orangeburg, SC 29115
B.A.

Clemson University
Dept. of Parks, Recreation, and
Tourism Mgmt.
Lehotsky Hall
Clemson, SC 29634-1005
B.S., MPRTM, M.S., Ph.D.

North Greenville College
Park and Recreation Program
P.O. Box 1892
Tigerville, NC 29688
B.A.

Yankton College
B.A.

South Dakota

Black Hills State College
B.A.

Northern State College
Recreation Curriculum
South Joy
Aberdeen, SD 57401
B.A.

South Dakota State University
HPER Dept.
Box 2829
Brookings, SD 57007
B.A.

University of South Dakota
B.A.

Tennessee

Austin Peay State University
Parks and Recreation Program
6012 College Street
Clarksville, TN 37044
B.A.

Belmont University
Park and Recreation Program
1900 Belmont Boulevard
Nashville, TN 37212-3757
B.A.

Bethel College
Park and Recreation Program
325 Cherry Avenue
McKenzie, TN 89201
B.A.

Carson Newman College
Dept. of HPELS
CNC Box 71897
Jefferson City, TN 37760
B.A.

Cumberland University
Recreation Dept.
S. Greenwood Street
Lebanon, TN 37087
B.A.

East Tennessee State University
Physical Education Dept.
P.O. Box 70654
Johnson City, TN 37614
B.A.

Fisk University
Recreation Dept.
1000 Seventeenth Avenue North
Nashville, TN 37208-3051
B.A.

Freed–Hardman University
Recreation Dept.
158 E. Main Street
Henderson, TN 38340

Lambuth University
Recreation Dept.
705 Lambuth Boulevard
Jackson, TN 38301
B.A.

Maryville College
Maryville, TN 37804
B.A.

Middle Tennessee State University
Recreation Program
Box 96
Murfreesboro, TN 37132
B.S. and M.S.

Tennessee State University
Recreation Dept.
Dixie Avenue
Cookeville, TN 38505
B.A.

University of Memphis
Recreation, Park, and Leisure
    Academic Dept. Human
    Movement, Science, and
    Education
Memphis, TN 38152
B.A., M.A.

University of Tennessee
Forestry Dept.
Cumberland Avenue
Knoxville, TN
B.A.

University of Tennessee,
    Chattanooga
Dept. of EHLS
615 McCallie Avenue
Chattanooga, TN 37403
B.A.

University of Tennessee,
    Knoxville
Recreation and Tourism Mgmt.
1914 Andy Holt Avenue
Knoxville, TN 37996-2710
B.S. and M.S.

University of Tennessee, Martin
Park and Recreation Admin.
Elam Center Rm. 1020
Martin, TN 38238
B.A.

Vanderbilt University
Campus Recreation
Box 6033, Station B
Nashville, TN 37235
B.A.

Texas

Baylor University
Leisure Services Division
P.O. Box 97313
Waco, TX 76798-7313
B.A.

Le Tourneau College
Longview, TX 75607
B.A.

San Antonio College
San Antonio, TX 78284
B.A.

Southwest Texas State University
Division of Recreation Admin.,
Dept. HPER
601 University Drive
San Marcos, TX 78666
B.A.

Stephen F. Austin State University
Nacogdoches, TX 75962
B.A.

Texas A&M University
Dept. of Recreation, Park, and
Tourism Sciences
College Station, TX 77843-
2261
B.S. in Recreation, Park, and
Tourism Sciences
M.S. and Ph.D. in Recreation,
Park, and Tourism Sciences
M.Agr. in Recreation and
Resources Development
M.Agr. in Natural Resources
Development

Texas Tech University
Box 4070
Lubbock, TX 79409
B.A., M.A., Ph.D.

Texas Technical University
Park Admin. and Landscape
Architecture
P.O. Box 4390
Lubbock, TX 79409
B.A., M.A.

Texas Woman's University
Denton, TX 76204
B.A.

University of North Texas
Dept. of Kinesiology, Health
Promotion, and Recreation
UNT Box 311337-PEB 209
Denton, TX 76203-1337
B.S. and M.S. in Recreation and
Leisure Studies

Utah

Brigham Young University
Dept. of Recreation Mgmt. and
Youth Leadership
Provo, UT 84602
B.S. in Leisure Services Mgmt.,
Therapeutic Recreation, and
Youth Leadership
M.S. in Recreation Mgmt.

University of Utah
Dept. of Parks, Recreation, and
Tourism
HPER-N 226
Salt Lake City, UT 84112
B.S., B.A. in Parks, Recreation,
and Tourism
M.S. in Parks, Recreation, and
Tourism
M. Phil., Ed.D., and Ph.D. in
Parks, Recreation, and
Tourism

Utah State University
Dept. of Health, Physical
Education, and Recreation
Logan, UT 84322-7000
B.S., M.A., Ph.D.

Utah State University
Forest Resources Dept.
5215 University Boulevard
Logan, UT 84322
B.A., M.A., Ph.D.

Vermont

Green Mountain College
Dept. of Recreation and
Leisure Studies
Poultney, VT 05764
B.S. in Therapeutic Recreation
B.S. in Recreation
B.S. in Leisure Resource
Facilities Mgmt.
B.S. in Adventure Recreation

Johnson State College
Business Mgmt. and Economics
Dept.
Johnson, VT 05656
B.A.

Lyndon State College
Dept. of Recreation Resource
and Ski Resort Mgmt.
Lyndonville, VT 05851
B.S. Recreation Resource and
Ski Resort Mgmt.

Norwich University
HPER Dept.
Northfield, VT 05663
B.A.

University of Vermont
Recreation Mgmt. Program
Aiken Center for Natural
Resources
Burlington, VT 05405-0088

Virginia

Christopher Newport University
Leisure Studies and Physical
Education
50 Shoe Lane
Newport News, VA 23606
B.A.

Eastern Mennonite College
Dept. of Physical Education and
Recreation
Harrisonburg, VA 22801
B.A.

Ferrum College
Recreation and Leisure Program
P.O. Box 1000
Ferrum, VA 24088
B.S. in Recreation and
Leisure–Generalists
B.S. in Outdoor Recreation

George Mason University
Parks Recreation and Leisure
Studies
10900 University Boulevard
Manassas, VA 20110
B.S.

Hampton University
Recreation Programming/TR
Holland Hall
Room 190
Hampton, VA 23668
B.A.

James Madison University
Health Sciences Dept.
Harrisonburg, VA 22807
B.A.

Longwood College
Dept. of Health, Physical
Education, Recreation, and
Dance
201 High Street
Farmville, VA 23909-1899
B.S. in Therapeutic Recreation

Lynchburg College
  Recreation Program
  Turner Gymnasium
  Lynchburg, VA 24501
  B.A.

Marymount College of Virginia
  Physical Fitness Mgmt.
  2807 North Glebe Road
  Arlington, VA 22207
  Associates, B.A.

Norfolk State University
  Norfolk, VA 23504
  B.A.

Old Dominion University
  Recreation and Leisure Studies
    Program
  Norfolk, VA 23529-0196
  B.S., M.S.

Radford University
  Dept. of Leisure Services
  Peters Hall
  Box 6963
  Radford, VA 24142
  B.S., B.A.

Shenandoah University
  Dept. of Physical Education and
    Recreation
  Singleton Gym
  Winchester, VA 22601
  B.A.

Virginia Commonwealth
    University
  Recreation, Parks, and Tourism
    Program
  817 W. Franklin Street
  P.O. Box 842015
  Richmond, VA 23284-2015
  B.S., M.S.

Virginia Polytechnic Institute
  Dept. of Forestry
  304 Cheatham
  Blacksburg, VA 24061-0324
  B.A., M.A., Ph.D.

Virginia State University
  Recreation Curriculum
  P.O. Box 66
  Petersburg, VA 23803
  B.A.

Virginia Union University
  Dept. of Recreation
  1500 N. Lombardy Street
  Richmond, VA 23220
  B.A.

Virginia Wesleyan College
  Dept. of Recreation and
    Leisure Studies
  Wesleyan Drive
  Norfolk, VA 23502
  B.A.

Washington
  Central Washington University
  Leisure Services Program
  400 E. Eighth Avenue
  Ellensburg, WA 98926
  B.A.

Centralia College
  B.A.

Clark College
  B.A.

Eastern Washington University
  Physical Education, Health,
    and Recreation Dept.
  MS #66
  526 Fifth Street
  Cheney, WA 99004
  B.A. in Recreation and Leisure
    Services

Gonzaga University
B.A.

Pacific Lutheran University
Tacoma, WA 98447
B.A.

Pierce College
B.A.

Skagit Valley College
Mount Vernon, WA 98273
B.A.

University of Washington
Seattle, WA 98195
B.A.

Washington State University
Recreation Admin. and Leisure
Studies
Smith Gym 208
Pullman, WA 99164-1410
B.A., M.A.

Washington State University
Wildlife Wildland Recreation
Mgmt.
Johnson Hall
Pullman, WA 99163
B.A., M.A.

Western Washington University
Recreation Program, HPER
Dept.
Old Carver #6
Bellingham, WA 98225-9067
B.A.

West Virginia
Alderson Broaddus College
Recreation Leadership
P.O. Box 547
Philippi, WV 26416
B.A.

Davis and Elkins College
Recreation Mgmt. and Tourism
Program
100 Sycamore Street
Elkins, WV 26241
B.A. in Recreation Mgmt. and
Tourism

Marshall University
Park Resources and Leisure
Services
Gullickson Hall
Huntington, WV 25755
B.S.

Shepherd College
Park Admin. Program
Shepherdstown, WV 25433
B.A.

Shepherd College
Recreation and Leisure Services
Shepherdstown, WV 25443
B.A.

West Virginia State College
Recreation Program, Dept. of
HPERS
Campus Box 8
Institute, WV 25112-1000
B.A.

West Virginia University
Recreation and Parks Mgmt.
P.O. Box 6125
Morgantown, WV 26506-6125
B.S.R. in Recreation
M.S.R. in Recreation

Wisconsin
Stratton College
B.A.

University of Wisconsin–La
  Crosse
Dept. of Recreation Mgmt. and
  Therapeutic Recreation
1128 Wittich Hall
La Crosse, WI 54601

University of Wisconsin,
  Milwaukee
Dept. of Human Kinetics
P.O. Box 413, Enderis Hall
Milwaukee, WI 53201

University of Wisconsin, River
  Falls
River Falls, WI 54022
B.A.

Wyoming

Central Wyoming College
Riverton, WY 82501
B.A.

University of Wyoming
Dept. of Geography and
  Recreation
P.O. Box 3371
Arts and Sciences Building
Laramie, WY 82071
B.S., M.S.

Western Wyoming College
B.A.

Canada

Alberta

Lakeland University
B.A.

Mount Royal College
B.A.

Red Deer College
Dept. of Recreation Admin.
Box 5005
Red Deer, AB T4N 5H5
Associates, B.A.

University of Alberta
B.A., M.A.

British Columbia

Capilano College
B.A.

Caribou College
B.A.

Malaspina University-College
Recreation Admin. and Tourism
  Studies
900 Fifth Street
Nanaimo, BC, V9R 1R7
2-year Diploma
  Program–Recreation Admin.,
  Tourism Studies
B.A. in Tourism, Combined
  Major Recreation Admin.

Selkirk College
B.A.

University of British Columbia
Park and Recreation Resources
270 MacMillan, 2357 Main
  Mall
Vancouver, BC V6T 1Z4

University of British Columbia
  Leisure and Sport Mgmt.,
    Human Kinetics
  Vancouver, BC V6T 1Z1

University of Northern British
    Columbia
  Resource Recreation and
    Tourism Program
  3333 University Way
  Prince George, BC, V2N 4Z9
  B.A., B.S.
  MSc. in Natural Resource
    Mgmt.
  M.A. in Natural Resource
    Mgmt.
  Ph.D. in Natural Resources
    Mgmt.

Manitoba

University of Manitoba
  Physical Education and
    Recreation Studies
  102 Frank Kennedy Centre
  Winnepeg, MB R3T 2N2
  B.S.

New Brunswick

College of Trades and Technology
  B.A.

Universite de Moncton
  CEPS Building
  Moncton, NB E1A 3E9
  B.A.

University of New Brunswick
  Physical Education and
    Recreation Faculty
  Fredericton, NB B3H 4H8
  B.A.

Newfoundland

Memorial University of
    Newfoundland
  School of Physical Education
    and Athletics
  St. John's, NF, A1C 5S7,
    Canada
  B.Rec.

Novia Scotia

Acadia University
  Wolfville, NS
  B.A., M.A.

Dalhousie University
  Halifax, NS
  B.A., M.A.

Ontario

Algonquin College
  B.A.

Brock University
  Recreation and Leisure Studies
  St. Catherine's, ON L2S 3A1
  B.A.

Canadore College
  B.A.

Centennial College
  B.A.

Conestoga College
  Recreation Leadership
  84 Frederick Street
  Kitchener, ON
  B.A.

Confederation College
  B.A.

Fanshawe College
 B.A.

Humber College
 B.A.

Lakehead University
 School of Outdoor Recreation
 Oliver Road
 Thunder Bay, ON P7B 5E1
 B.A.

Mowhawk College
 B.A.

University of Ottawa
 Dept. of Leisure Studies
 550 Cumberland Street
 Ottawa, ON K1N 6N5
 B.A.

University of Waterloo
 Waterloo, ON B2L 3G1
 B.A., M.A., Ph.D.

York University
 Wellness Program
 274 Vanier North
 York, ON M3J 1P3
 B.A.

Quebec

College de Riviere du Loup
 B.A.

Concordia University
 Dept. of Leisure Studies
 7141 Sherbrooke St. W.
 Montreal, Quebec, H4B 1R6

Universite Du Quebec A Trois-
  Rivieres
 Dept. of Leisure Studies and
  Communication Pavillion
  Ringuet
 C. P. 500
 Trois-Rivieres, Quebec,
  G9A 5H7
 B.S. in Recreology
 M.S. in Leisure, Culture, and
  Tourism

Saskatchewan
 University of Regina
 Regina, SK
 B.A.

University of Saskatchewan
 B.A., M.A.

CHAPTER 6

WHERE TO FIND A JOB

In the past, the public was accustomed to relying on volunteers for recreation leadership. Now, the new millennium brings with it the realization that these recreation professionals are available resources and are deserving of monetary rewards for their hard work. Recreation professionals are now being employed at all levels of government. Federal and state government positions are not as numerous as jobs in local governments, but they have increased significantly in recent years. It appears that the number of federal and state positions will remain fairly stable in the near future because of public pressure not to expand government services and to decrease the escalation of government spending.

Local government positions in city, county, and district recreation agencies constitute a major source of employment ranging all the way from direct leaders to departmental administrators. Increasingly professionals are becoming employed by such commercial recreation enterprises as private golf courses, ski resorts, tennis clubs, theme parks, private camps, beach and boating resorts, sports clubs, health spas, and housing and condominium complexes. Other agencies that employ recreation leaders with specific qualifications are hospitals (therapeutic recreation), correctional institutions, the military, industrial organizations, and voluntary youth service agencies.

FEDERAL GOVERNMENT EMPLOYMENT

In the past most federal agencies have given primary attention to graduates whose educational emphasis was in the biological sciences; however, personnel with majors in recreation, social science, physical science, liberal arts, physical education, landscape architecture, and engineering also have been hired. The present philosophy of government administrators seems to favor personnel with dual talents who can effectively relate people to resource settings. They want professionals who are competent in working with all kinds of natural and man-made areas to make the best use of their aesthetic, functional, and economic potential. But more importantly, the professionals must always be aware that the areas are for people.

Opportunities for employment with the Heritage Conservation and Recreation Service (HCRS, formerly the Bureau of Outdoor Recreation) primarily are available to those who qualify as outdoor recreation planners. Typically, HCRS planners make studies of recreation resource needs, prepare recommendations of transportation proposals, evaluate federal land acquisition programs, review and comment on federal environmental statements, evaluate state comprehensive outdoor recreation plans, consult with state officials on outdoor recreation programs, and evaluate requests for financial assistance provided through federal funds under the Land and Water Conservation Fund Act. The HCRS does not manage any natural resources, nor does it direct any activity-oriented programs. It is primarily an agency for coordinating, planning, and financing public outdoor recreation.

In the recruitment of employees, the HCRS seeks candidates who have completed a four-year course of study leading to an appropriate bachelor's degree from an accredited college or university in areas of biological sciences, natural resource management and conservation, social science, design and planning, earth science, or outdoor recreation. Eligibility for appointment to the HCRS staff is dependent upon the candidate's performance on the Professional and Administrative Career Examination (PACE), which is administered by the Civil Service. New entries into the HCRS are hired with the Civil Service ratings of GS-5 and GS-7. When a vacancy occurs, the service requests from the Civil Service Commission (CSC) a list of eligible candidates from the PACE examination list.

Information about taking the examination may be obtained from your local post office or any CSC office. Additional information about employment opportunities with HCRS may be obtained from the HCRS headquarters, Department of the Interior Building, Washington, DC, or from any of the seven HCRS regional offices.

The National Park Service (NPS) has a permanent staff of more than seven thousand year-round employees, managing almost 340 national park areas throughout the nation. For those entering the NPS, employment opportunities are available in the following positions: park ranger, park naturalist, historian, archaeologist, and designer. The administrative positions are held by long-time NPS employees. The Park Service hires numerous summer employees, and a person contemplating a National Park Service career ought to have at least one summer of Park Service employment while pursuing his or her education.

Like the HCRS, the NPS selects its employees from the Civil Service Commission's list of candidates who have scored high on the PACE.

Interested applicants may obtain a copy of the examination announcement covering the position in which they are interested at the local post office, at an office of the Civil Service Commission, or by writing the NPS Headquarters, Department of the Interior, Washington, DC.

The U.S. Forest Service, a division of the Department of Agriculture, employs a large number of resource management personnel. A small proportion of these employees are involved primarily in the planning and management of outdoor recreation. Schools of forestry at several universities now offer specialization in outdoor recreation (see list in Chapter 5), and the graduates of these programs constitute the main source of recreation personnel hired by the U.S. Forest Service. With the national forests being used more and more for recreation, there will continue to be a steady increase in demand for competent forest recreation personnel. Like the HCRS and NPS, the Forest Service selects its employees from candidates identified through the Civil Service Commission. Information about examination procedures may be obtained from the local post office, from any district or regional forest service office, or by writing directly to the U.S. Forest Service, Department of Agriculture, Washington, DC.

Other federal agencies that offer limited opportunities for employment in outdoor recreation are The U.S. Fish and Wildlife Service, The Bureau of Reclamation, The U.S. Army Corps of Engineers, The Bureau of Land Management, and The Tennessee Valley Authority. All of these are large resource management agencies whose areas receive extensive recreational use by the public. Therefore, recreation planning and management have become the responsibility of each of these agencies.

STATE GOVERNMENT POSITIONS

A few decades ago the state park systems were meager in most states and received relatively few visitors. In 1960, state parks numbered 1,900 and received 100 million visitors; by 1970, the number of parks had increased to 2,800, receiving 310 million visitors annually. By the 1990s, there were approximately 3,800 state parks with well over 500 million annual visits. This trend is indicative of demands being placed on state fish and wildlife divisions, natural resource management agencies, and other divisions of state governments involved in outdoor resource management.

In recent years our better and more popular recreation areas have been strained to the limit. Federal and state legislators have recognized this and have taken rather bold measures to correct the situation through development of areas and employment of more individuals better qualified in leadership.

Every state has a department that manages the state park system, and some of these departments also offer recreation consultation services. Additionally, every state has a wildlife management agency and departments or divisions that manage other state-owned natural resources. Further, every state has a tourism office and a designated person or office that coordinates the state's recreation functions with the Federal Heritage Conservation and Recreation Service.

Some, but not all, of the personnel in these state departments and divisions are prepared professionally in recreation. Despite the fact that these jobs are not the exclusive domain of recreation professionals, there are several agencies in state governments that have significant responsibilities in recreation, providing some opportunities for employment of specialists in the field.

By reviewing the responsibilities of the agencies named, it becomes apparent that most of the recreation-related positions are in outdoor recreation or natural resource-related recreation. The positions are relatively few in each state, with the more populated states generally providing better employment opportunities. Most state positions of this kind are filled by applicants processed through the State Civil Service Office. However, it is beneficial to also contact the particular department of government where you wish to be employed to be sure that your interests and qualifications are known. Applications and announcements are available at employment offices or by contacting your local state Civil Service office.

LOCAL GOVERNMENT OPPORTUNITIES

Local government recreation leaders can be divided into four general categories: *administrators* (executives), *supervisors, center or special facility directors,* and *direct leaders.*

Administrative Positions. These positions involve planning, organizing, and administering a recreation and/or park program to meet the needs and interests of those being served. The title might be *manager, director, superintendent,* or *executive.* Most administrators are responsible for both recreation programming and park management; however, sometimes these two major responsibilities are placed under separate administrators. Typically the responsibilities of the administrator include the following:

- Administer work of the department in accordance with prescribed policies and basic procedures that usually are established by a governing board or commission.
- Recruit, select, assign, supervise, and evaluate the departmental staff.
- Oversee the acquisition, planning, construction, improvement, and maintenance of areas and facilities.
- Prepare the annual budget proposal, administer the budget, and account for all revenues and expenditures.

- Give leadership to the public relations efforts of the department.
- Provide administrative guidance to supervisors and center directors to be sure their phases of the program are managed effectively.
- Arrange in-service training to improve the performance of staff members.
- Instigate, support, and evaluate research studies relating to the departmental operation.
- Motivate and inspire departmental personnel.

The required training of an administrator varies considerably with the size and complexity of the department. But usually it includes graduation from a recognized college or university with at least a bachelor's degree in recreation administration, park management, or some closely related field, plus successful experience over a period of several years. A graduate degree is often helpful and sometimes required. Substantial evidence of a sound philosophy and superior management ability outweigh most other considerations.

Supervisory Positions. Representing a secondary level of administration, supervisors are responsible for all of the activities and/or facilities within a specific geographic area (general supervisor) or for a specialized area of the program (special supervisor). A *supervisor of a district* would be responsible for the administration of all or specified portions of the recreation program and facilities in that geographic district. The responsibilities would be very similar to those of the department administrator except the supervisor's responsibilities would pertain only to a portion of the community. A *special supervisor* would be responsible for a specialized phase of the program, such as athletics, aquatics, or social activities. Usually a department would not have both general (geographic) supervisors and special (activity) supervisors, but would have one or the other. However, in some large departments there are supervisors of both kinds.

Normally the qualifications for supervisors include a bachelor's degree in recreation or a closely related field, along with a specified period of experience.

Directors of Centers and Special Facilities. A community or neighborhood center is a multipurpose recreation complex that needs to be under the leadership of an administrator who is effective in promotion, programming, and working with people, particularly the residents and individuals in the vicinity of the center. The director is in charge of the staff and the facility and is charged with the responsibility of utilizing these effectively to accomplish the purposes of the center. Ordinarily the director is responsible to an area supervisor or to the department administrator.

Another kind of director is the one placed in charge of a special facility or a facility more singular in purpose than a neighborhood center such as a botanical garden, a zoo, a waterfront area, a museum, or a cultural center. A person holding one of these positions is usually a specialist in the particular area of interest for which the center is designed. Here again, the director would be responsible for using the staff, facilities, and other resources as effectively as possible to accomplish the purposes of the special center.

Direct Leaders. Direct leaders are those who furnish face-to-face leadership to people. Direct leaders have such responsibilities as organizing and directing athletic contests, directing aquatics programs, teaching dance, preparing concerts and recitals, promoting and directing dramatics productions, and leading children in playground activities.

For full-time direct leadership positions, a college degree in recreation or a related field is generally required; two years of college study give sufficient preparation for certain positions while a degree from a four-year college or university is usually required for most upper-level management positions. Part-time or summer jobs often are filled by college students who have the particular qualifications needed or by teachers who enjoy this kind of summer employment.

COLLEGE TEACHING

According to the National Recreation and Parks Association, in 1967, 809 faculty were employed to prepare the 2,070 graduates of college recreation curricula. Almost half of these teachers taught a portion of their load in other departments, or taught only part-time at the college while engaging in other professional work. It is assumed that the number of faculty members increases approximately in proportion to the number of graduates, meaning that in 1990, there were approximately 7,000 college and university faculty members involved in recreation and park curricula on either a full-time or part-time basis.

In order to qualify for a college teaching position, two or more years of highly successful professional experience are required along with at least a master's degree. Today a person holding a doctoral degree has a distinct advantage in the competition for college faculty positions.

RECREATION THERAPY

Numerous hospitals of various kinds have recreation therapy programs, particularly mental, veterans, and children's hospitals. Such programs are based on the philosophy that people confined to hospitals for long periods of time need and benefit from participation in wholesome and interesting leisure time activities. The programs are designed to encourage positive attitudes and high morale among the patients while developing their personalities.

The smaller hospitals often have only one recreation specialist on the staff while some of the larger hospitals have several specialists, with one of them serving as coordinator or supervisor of the program. Many of the hospitals are owned by either the state or federal government, such as state mental hospitals and federal veteran hospitals. In such cases, the employment conditions of recreation therapists are defined by Civil Service specifications. Such employment can be investigated by contacting the state Civil Service office or the office directly in charge of the recreation therapy program at a particular hospital.

Those seeking recreation therapy positions need to prepare themselves by completing a specialized program in this field at a four-year college or university. (A few positions are available for people who have completed an associate or two-year college program.) Also, most positions require a Certified Therapeutic Recreation Specialist (CTRS) certification. For those who want additional training beyond a bachelor's degree, several institutions offer specialized preparation at the master's degree level.

Relatively speaking, therapeutic recreation has been one of the fastest growing areas of professional recreation in recent years. There is a limitation on the number of professionals that can be accommodated in this field because of the restricted hospital population. But different locations are appearing in the private sector and opening consulting firms is always an option.

Working with hospital patients is extremely satisfying to some people while others cannot adapt to it. In trying to determine whether this type of employment is for you, it is important to analyze your own personality to determine whether you would fit the mold. Hospital field experience early in your professional training program can be valuable in helping you decide whether this is the field for you.

INDUSTRIAL RECREATION

Certain industrial organizations or plants provide a recreation program for employees and dependents as part of the employee benefits. Or sometimes the program is sponsored by the employees' organization, usually known as an association or club. Industrial recreation agencies often own such specialized facilities as a private park, a golf course, or a hunting club. Such programs involve a variety of leagues and tournaments designed to furnish participation opportunities to employees and family members in interesting and developmental activities. The exact responsibilities and working conditions of industrial recreation leaders vary from each other considerably because each industrial organization is independent and different from any other. Further, the norms for professional qualifications and working conditions are less defined in this area of recreation than in most others. Anyone interested in entering this field of employment should contact the National Industrial Recreation Association at 20 North Wacker Drive, Chicago, IL 60606.

ARMED FORCES RECREATION

Ever since World War II, the Armed Forces have been committed to providing ample recreational opportunities for military personnel and their dependents. The recreation leadership positions are filled by a combination of military personnel and civil service employees, with certain of the positions being clearly identified as Civil Service jobs. Most such positions are within the United States but there are some opportunities at U.S. military stations in foreign countries. A person entering this field would normally receive a GS-5 or GS-7 rating; however, higher ratings are possible for people who have had extensive professional experience. For those interested in this form of employment, the best sources of specific information are the nearest Civil Service Commission office or the Division of Special Services of the particular military branch at the headquarters of that branch of service in Washington, DC (i.e., Department of the Army).

EMPLOYMENT BY PRIVATE CLUBS

Recreation leadership positions in private clubs come in a variety of forms. For example, the same club might employ a golf professional primarily as a teacher, an aquatics specialist to oversee the swimming program, and a clubhouse manager to oversee a variety of activities for the clubhouse. Other kinds of private clubs providing employment opportunities are tennis clubs, swim clubs, gun clubs, and health clubs (or health spas). Success in most of these positions is dependent upon a high level of skill in the particular activity involved along with an appealing personality that will attract and hold clientele over an extended period of time. For example, a golf or tennis pro must have a reputation as a performer that will give him or her entry into a pro position and cause people to want to perpetuate him or her in that position. Of course, success over a period of time will be dependent upon how effectively the pro performs all aspects of the duties in that position.

COMMERCIAL RECREATION POSITIONS

As in any business, commercial recreation is based upon a free enterprise system in which the individual or company prepares and distributes services and products in an effort to make a profit. This fact of business life (operating at a profit) forces the successful operator to remain sensitive and responsive to the public being served.

Job opportunities in commercial recreation are quite varied and traditionally have been relatively sparse. However, it is becoming ever more apparent that the increasing recreation needs of Americans will not be met effectively in the future by the combined efforts of local, state, and federal government agencies. This will result in increased opportunities in commercial recreation.

Jobs in this field include such positions as manager of a boys' or girls' ranch; manager or guide for a wilderness tour or expedition organization; employee of a recreation travel agency; manager of a bowling alley or an amusement park; manager or employee of an outdoor recreation enterprise; private consultant for the planning of recreation areas, facilities, and programs; manager or employee of a commercial waterfront or ski resort, an aquatics center, or a skating rink.

The success of commercial recreation enterprises and the personnel involved with them varies from very poor to highly successful, just as in other kinds of businesses. Those going into commercial recreation need to be somewhat cautious and plan very carefully with respect to investment as compared to potential return. In addition, certain characteristics and abilities are vital to a successful entrepreneur. He or she must be able to meet the public effectively, have some ability as a personnel and financial manager, possess ingenuity and creativity, and have the ability for self-promotion. Included in one's preparation should be some carefully selected courses in business management and business procedures.

Commercial recreation firms that qualify can obtain federal financial assistance (low interest loans) and planning assistance through the Small Business Administration and the Farmer's Home Administration. Also, certain states have assistance programs available to recreation and tourism enterprises.

TOURISM

The total travel industry is much broader than just its recreational aspects. However, travel for pleasure is a very significant part of the industry and therefore should be identified as a field of recreational employment opportunity. It is interesting that in forty-six of the fifty states, tourism ranks as one of the top three industries. This would seem to imply a gigantic number of job opportunities, but one should not be overly optimistic about this because most tourists travel by private automobile and make their own travel arrangements. However, about 20 percent of the tourist travel occurs on airlines, buses, and trains, and a good portion of this involves organized tours. These tours may be sponsored and organized by nonprofit groups such as schools and religious, political, cultural, civic, professional, and community organizations.

Those employed in the tourist industry are involved mainly in arranging transportation, food and lodging, and entertainment. Anyone interested in tourism job opportunities needs to be interested in and prepared for promotional work, business management, personnel management, and public relations. The state office of tourism (every state has one) would be a good place to obtain specific information about tourism statistics and trends.

OUTDOOR EDUCATION

This occupational field is closely related to outdoor recreation but is separate in the sense that outdoor education in the schools is a branch of education requiring a teaching certificate. Those interested in this field ordinarily would qualify by pursuing a program in outdoor education, which would typically be offered through the College of Education. Upon completion, the person would seek employment with a school district as an outdoor education specialist.

There are less formal approaches to outdoor education that offer a limited number of opportunities. For example, a few cities and some federal agencies manage outdoor education or interpretative centers where employees are specialists in outdoor education but are not necessarily certified to teach in a school system.

For anyone interested in outdoor education, a good source of specific information is the Director, Outdoor Education Project, American Alliance for Health, Physical Education, Recreation, and Dance, 1900 Association Drive, Reston, VA, 22091.

RESOURCE MANAGEMENT

Approximately 5 percent of the 2.3 billion acres of land that comprise the fifty United States is designated primarily for parks, recreation, wildlife refuges, and public institutions and facilities. The management and effective utilization and preservation of this land with its complex soil, plant, and animal systems combined with people's desire for recreation and beauty opens up a variety of important career opportunities.

Positions in the natural resource management field include foresters to manage, develop, and protect wildlands and their resources; forestry aids and technicians to assist the forester with timber sales, supervise recreation area use, and be involved with public education, fire prevention, and research activities; range managers to develop, protect, and plan for the use of the one billion acres of rangeland in the United States including recreation, grazing, timber, and watersheds; soil conservationists to plan, apply, and maintain programs for soil and water conservation, utilization, and treatment; wildlife conservationists to manipulate our soil, water, plants, and animals so as to produce the desired number of animals based on the best interests of humanity; and fishery conservationists to manage our commercial and sports fisheries, which supply and promote more than six hundred million recreation days per year in this country.

Those individuals interested in resource management are encouraged to take courses such as natural resource management, wildlife management, environmental interpretations, and outdoor systems management. It would also be desirable to seek summer employment during undergraduate preparation and seek meaningful fieldwork or internship experience before seeking a job.

For further information, apply to the Soil Conservation Service, the Heritage Conservation and Recreation Service, the regional office of the U.S. Forest Service, the National Park Service, the Fish and Wildlife Service, the Bureau of Land Management, or other appropriate agencies.

EMPLOYMENT CONDITIONS

In the future, leisure time career opportunities within the broad spectrum of parks, recreation, and conservation will involve critical issues ranging from the inner ghettos to the wilderness of the great outdoors, and from face-to-face interaction with people to the less personal but equally meaningful elements of rivers and forests. In every instance, regardless of the special interest area pursued, *people* will be the ultimate beneficiaries. The leaders and workers who give direction and impetus to this vast effort will come from many walks of life, and they will be involved in a variety of ways. The following discussion will help you gain insight into present and future opportunities and working conditions in recreation and parks professions.

WOMEN AND MINORITIES

Approximately 40 percent of the college students majoring in recreation and park curricula are women. Employment opportunities for women are good. A woman who is well qualified for this field of work will find plenty of opportunity for gainful employment if she is willing to locate herself in the areas where the opportunities exist.

In the past, employment of minorities in the field of recreation has been concentrated in large cities but is becoming more widespread.

Federal agencies are bound by law to give equal opportunity to members of minority groups and to women. The same requirements for equal opportunities exist in state government. The recreation occupations reflect this trend toward equal employment opportunities for persons of commensurate abilities, and salaries for women and members of minority groups are also required by law to be the same as salaries for other employees in parallel positions.

THE DISADVANTAGED

In addition to planning programs and services for the population as a whole, substantial effort must be directed toward special population groups whose needs are related to economic inadequacies and/or environmental deficiencies. Very often the culturally, educationally, and economically disadvantaged are the same individuals who are recreationally disadvantaged. Therefore, to some degree, they lack opportunities for preparing themselves to become effective leaders in recreational programs. However, there are many individual exceptions to this. Further, some program administrators arrange workshops and clinics to help prospective disadvantaged employees to overcome their deficiencies. Most of this needs to be done.

Employment of the disadvantaged is especially relevant to the park and recreation field because the recreation leader must be able to understand the problems of the neighborhood and community and to communicate with the residents. Ethnic and racial balance in personnel greatly enhances the effectiveness of local park and recreation systems.

The NRPA and AAHPERD conducted a survey of 980 agencies throughout the United States to determine the number of disadvantaged workers in local public park and recreation agencies. Twenty-one distinct job classifications were listed. The survey revealed that disadvantaged workers hold approximately 13 percent of the full-time jobs in parks and recreation and 25 percent of the part-time positions, most of which are seasonal jobs.

More than half of the disadvantaged workers employed in park and recreation agencies were in occupational categories of semi- or nonskilled personnel, such as facility supervisor, semiskilled park personnel, attendants and aides, and certain clerical positions. Of those occupying part-time and seasonal positions, the majority were in the category of attendants and aides. When the information from this study was compared to the information from a similar study done earlier (1967), the comparison showed a substantial employment increase in the categories of recreation program leaders, attendants and aides, activity specialists, facility supervisors, and park rangers. In the same study it was found that a little more than 1 percent of park and recreation employees are handicapped. Of these, about three out of ten are professionals, while the other seven out of ten are in nonprofessional jobs.

GENERALIST OR SPECIALIST

As indicated, there are certain positions in this field that require a high degree of specialization, whereas other positions require more generalized preparation. Whether you should prepare to be a specialist or a generalist depends on the nature of the position to which you aspire. Obviously, if you want to be a golf or tennis pro or teach fitness or do leisure counseling, you must be a specialist of the highest order and generalized preparation is only a supplementary value. Conversely, if you are preparing to be a recreation supervisor or eventually the director of a program, generalized preparation covering a broad scope of the field would give you a stronger base for achieving your aspirations. The earlier in your professional preparation you can decide what you want to accomplish in your profession and on what time schedule, the better prepared you will be to determine the degree of specialization or generalization you should pursue. There are places in this field for both generalists and specialists but these two kinds of employment require quite different preparation and experience.

SALARIES

Salaries relating to specific situations are stated in the descriptions of the case studies that follow in Chapter 7, but this additional information will help you to have a better overview of the salary situation. Salaries for full-time recreation positions range from approximately $12,000 to more than $70,000 per year. This is understandable because of the great variety of positions in this field. The salary scale for positions in municipal programs (the largest employment area in recreation) parallel rather closely the salaries for public school teachers in the same geographic area. This means that beginning salaries for employees with a bachelor's degree would range from $15,000 to $30,000 for eleven months. Jobs with youth agencies and hospitals also parallel teaching salaries rather closely.

Those employed by the federal government in recreation positions would receive salaries comparable to other federal employees of the same experience and rating. These are civil service jobs, and the salaries are determined by the civil service pay scale. Generally, federal employees in the field of recreation would receive between $18,000 and $40,000 per year. A few of the top positions would pay more. Recreationists employed in state government positions would also receive salaries comparable to their counterparts at the state level. Typically, state government employees receive $1,000 to $2,000 less per year than their federal government counterparts.

Faculty members in university recreation departments have salaries that cover the range of university faculty members in general. A typical salary for a young teacher with a master's degree and the rank of instructor would be $26,000 per year. A middle-aged teacher with a doctoral degree and the rank of associate professor would earn about $35,000. A professionally mature and expert faculty member holding a doctor's degree and the rank of a full professor will earn $40,000 or more per year. Department heads of some of the better recognized departments would receive several thousand per year more than this.

The highest paid people in the profession are the executives of large municipal programs. The one in charge of the program in a city of one million population, for example, would receive a salary of more than $55,000.

The summer salaries of student employees would be $5.00 to $10.00 per hour, and the same would be true for year-round part-time employees. However, summer positions that pay considerably better than this are available to better prepared employees, such as school teachers.

Commercial recreation positions are the most difficult to interpret from the standpoint of salary expectations. These are like other private enterprise positions, meaning that the salary and the future success of the employee depend largely on the profit margin and the stability of the organization.

A WORD OF CAUTION

Even though the future of the recreation and park profession appears generally bright, it is important to understand that this field does not present a plethora of employment opportunities. It will undoubtedly experience consistent growth and the profession will gain improved status, but the growth and improvement will not be as ultra-dramatic as some have predicted.

During the past decade the market for college trained recreation and park personnel has expanded at a steady and healthy rate, and there is no reason to expect that this trend will change. In view of the recent past the following points are important: (1) Those who want to make a career of this field need to prepare themselves expertly so they can compete in the job market, and (2) the leaders of the profession need to strive for more effective development and enforcement of standards and procedures that will enhance the employment of those who have prepared themselves well for leadership positions.

CHAPTER 7

PERSONAL STORIES OF PEOPLE WORKING IN THE FIELD

> Leisure is intrinsically bound up in the quality of life. Its distribution—among the population and over lifetimes—and the uses to which it is put are indicative of the well-being of a society. Yet the growth of available leisure time in this country has been less widely noted than a corresponding growth in the output of goods and services, perhaps because of its elusive quality.
>
> J. D. Hodgson, former Secretary of Labor

The following are descriptions of typical situations in which individuals have been successful in leisure time occupations. These success stories purposely cover a broad range of jobs and exemplify various avenues by which people become employed in recreation-related positions. There are many other examples that could be cited but these give a fairly broad spectrum of the leadership opportunities in this field. Keep in mind that these are success stories; other stories could be told that would illustrate lack of success.

According to the *Occupational Outlook Handbook,* median annual earnings of recreation workers who worked full-time in 1996 were about $18,700, significantly lower than the median of $25,600 for workers in all occupations. The middle 50 percent earned between about $12,900 and $28,900, while the top 10 percent earned $37,500 or more. However, earnings of recreation directors and others in supervisory or managerial positions can be substantially higher.

Most public and private recreation agencies provide full-time recreation workers with typical benefits; part-time workers receive few, if any, benefits.

William Freeman is assistant director of a state parks department in a western state that administers approximately seventy-six state park and recreation areas. He is a state civil service employee with over sixteen years of tenure with the State Parks Department and has been assistant director for about ten years. Mr. Freeman holds a bachelor's degree in recreation and park planning and a master's degree in public administration. Before his employment by the state, he had several years of experience as an employee of a ski resort during the winter months.

Paul Pearson is the director of recreation for a community of approximately twenty-seven thousand. During the summer, the municipal program is expanded to include a large variety of activities with emphasis on youth, and numerous part time employees are hired. During the school year, the program is reduced to a more minimal level with a small staff. Mr. Pearson has the same fringe benefits as other city employees. Prior to his present position, he was a physical education teacher and athletic coach in the public schools. Mr. Pearson holds a bachelor's degree in physical education and a master's degree in recreation administration. It was after obtaining the master's degree that he moved from education into recreation administration.

Margaret Murphy is a faculty member in the Department of Recreation and Park Administration at a university in the Midwest. She holds the rank of associate professor. Prior to becoming a university professor, Margaret Murphy had three years of experience on the staff of a youth service agency, was on the staff of a community center for two years, and was a supervisor in a municipal recreation program for two years. During her undergraduate college years she had summer employment in a youth camp and a municipal recreation program. Professor Murphy has completed bachelor's, master's, and doctorate degrees. She is an energetic and cheerful person, and she keeps well informed on facts and concepts relating to her profession. To enhance her professional preparation and overall contributions, she has kept active in professional organizations and community affairs.

Sema Nicholic currently is employed as the tennis professional (head instructor) at a private tennis club in Florida. He came to the United States in 1968 from Yugoslavia to attend college on a tennis scholarship. He spent four years as a successful member of the tennis team while improving his skill in the English language and earning a bachelor's degree in a noncertification physical education program. Upon graduation he accepted a job as an assistant tennis pro at a private club in Georgia. After two years of experience and proving himself as an excellent instructor and a good organizer, he accepted the head pro position at the club in Florida at a substantial increase in salary. It seems likely that Nicholic will continue along this line of employment, and by doing so, he will accomplish two important purposes: he will earn a very good living in a leisure time occupation, and he will contribute much to the enjoyment and enrichment of those he teaches.

Dennis Marshall is supervisor of a recreation program sponsored by the employee association of a large industrial plant in Nashville, Tennessee. The association owns various facilities, including a family-youth camp forty miles away and a park located near the industrial complex, which includes a clubhouse, swimming facilities, athletic fields, and picnic areas. In addition to the activities sponsored at these two privately owned facilities, the program includes participation in such instructional and competitive activities as bowling and skating. Mr. Marshall became familiar with this position through his involvement as an industrial employee while working his way through college. Being a recreation major, he showed strong interest and inclination toward recreation leadership at the plant. Upon graduation from college, he was able to work part-time in the plant while working as an assistant in the recreation program. After two years of this arrangement, he became director of the industrial recreation program. Even though he is an employee of the association and not the industrial organization, arrangements have been made for him to receive all of the fringe benefits available to the industrial employees. Even though Mr. Marshall's present job does not offer great opportunity for advancement, it is a substantial position that offers a good future. Further, it is providing good preparation for moving to more lucrative employment of the same kind with another organization.

Ilene Parker is a civilian recreation employee at a naval base on the West Coast, holding a civil service rating of GS-7. Having served as a recreation employee with the Armed Forces for eleven years, she has been on the staff at three different military stations—two in the United States and one in Europe. She has desirable fringe benefits and a bright future with the federal service. Prior to entering civil service employment, Ms. Parker worked in a municipal recreation program, first as an activities specialist, then as a recreation center director, and later as supervisor of a geographic region within the municipal program.

Mike Ranier is the golf pro at a medium-sized golf club in northern California. After spending a great deal of time during his teenage years learning the game and developing a high level of skill, Ranier gained entrance onto a university golf team where he perfected his game and learned much about instructional techniques. He earned a bachelor's degree with a major in business management with the idea that he would pursue golf instruction and golf course management as his profession. He supplements his salary with additional funds as a consultant and by playing in local tournaments.

Lyon Allredge, assistant superintendent of schools in an Arizona community of approximately 210,000, has the specific responsibility of administering the community school program. This program is based on the concept of making thorough community use of school facilities. Much of the use is in the form of recreational activities during out-of-school hours. Mr. Allredge obtained a bachelor's degree in education and taught in the public schools for three years before returning to the university where he earned a master's degree in community school administration. His future appears bright because his position is stable, his future salary will be in accordance with the local school district pay scale, and the fringe benefits and working conditions are desirable. In the future, he may find opportunity to move to a similar position in a larger organization, or he might someday become a school principal or the superintendent of schools in his present community.

John Martin is a director of a private swim club in Philadelphia. Having been an outstanding competitive swimmer, his reputation and demonstrated competency attract a sufficient clientele within the membership of the club to sustain the program at a high level. In addition to earning a bachelor's degree with a major in physical education, he has had extensive experience in swimming competition and in teaching and training younger competitors. After graduation from college, Mr. Martin worked for two years as an assistant in a privately owned commercial swim school, after which he had two years experience as a college swim coach. The future looks bright for him with respect to both earnings and professional status.

Robert Saffrine is stationed at Teuton National Park in Jackson, Wyoming, as a park planner employed with the National Park Service. His bachelor's degree was in landscape architecture and horticulture, and he has been employed with the Park Service with a civil service rating of GS-8. He enjoys all the fringe benefits associated with civil service employment, in addition to the benefit of low-rent federal housing. Being a dedicated outdoorsman and an advocate of preservation and conservative use of natural resources for the enjoyment of people, Mr. Saffrine is pleased with his contribution to society and finds his work very satisfying. At a relatively young age he is well established with the federal service and plans to continue as a National Park employee.

Evan Stephenson is a director of a college student union on the campus of a state university with a student body of about ninety-five hundred. Management of the student union includes food services, a student union activities program, and student body officer leadership. Mr. Stephenson earned a bachelor's degree in sociology and, after three years of employment as a social worker, went back to college and earned a master's degree in recreation administration. Following two years' experience as a teacher on the recreational faculty at a junior college, he accepted his present position. He has the potential of a good future in his present position or the possibility of moving into a higher level management position at the university. His fringe benefits are the same as those of other university employees.

George Eubank is an aggressive and ambitious young man who taught on a university faculty for two years following graduation from a master's degree program. After deciding not to make a career of teaching, he entered the commercial recreation field as a limited partner and assistant manager of Outdoor Recreation Unlimited, a regional hunting and fishing organization. ORU conducts hunting and fishing excursions, provides guide services, and sells memberships to people who want to hunt and fish on private lands where the organization has leased hunting and fishing rights. As in other private enterprises, Mr. Eubanks will rise or fall with the success of the organization. Therefore, he must help the organization produce a profit on a regular basis while at the same time building its assets so it will become a more substantial enterprise. His job is primarily planning and promotional in nature.

Paul Allen is presently a district representative for a sports and recreation equipment and supply company. He graduated from college with undergraduate training in the areas of recreation and sociology; after working three years in a municipal recreation program, he returned to college and earned a master's degree in park and recreation administration. He then joined the State Extension Service at a land grant university in the capacity of recreation and park specialist. After serving in this position for four years, he accepted his present position, which he finds his exciting and challenging, and he believes it offers a very promising financial future.

Susan Jolley is an aquatic specialist who works in a municipal swim program. She graduated with an associate degree in recreation from a nearby junior college. Because of her long-time interest and participation in aquatic activities, including competitive swimming, she is well qualified as a swimming instructor and as a supervisor of aquatics. As a full-time employee, she has the same fringe benefits as other city employees. She is married and contemplates raising a family, and she plans to continue full-time employment.

Myron Hogan is the grounds supervisor of a large city park in a populous area. Mr. Hogan holds an associate degree in horticulture from a community college and, prior to obtaining his present position, he worked with the city parks department as a park maintenance man. It was during this time that he went to college part-time and earned the associate degree.

Trina Peligreno is a recreation therapist in a veterans' hospital in the eastern seaboard region. Ms. Peligreno earned a bachelor's degree from a state college in New York with a major in pre-physical therapy. Rather than going to a physical therapy school, she decided to earn a master's degree in recreation therapy. Extending her master's degree education over a two-year period, she was able to work part-time as a recreation aide in a children's hospital. Upon completion of the degree, she was employed full-time for two years at the children's hospital as a recreation therapist before joining the staff at the veterans' hospital three years ago. Ms. Peligreno thoroughly enjoys working with hospital patients, and she feels she serves an excellent purpose in adding interest to their lives and helping with their rehabilitation.

George Adamson is a superintendent of recreation and parks for a city in the Midwest of approximately a half million people. He has had a variety of experience in the profession. He was a school teacher for two years, then took a job in the recreation field, earning a master's degree while continuing full-time employment. In his present position, he administers a program that employs a full-time year-round staff of 150 workers. He enjoys the desirable fringe benefits of administrative employees. Mr. Adamson has had a very significant influence on the development of his community and is well known and respected in the city. In addition, he is well known in the profession and has had significant influence on its development at both the regional and national levels.

Jan Eliason is an employee of a recreation travel agency that promotes and schedules various kinds of excursions, including river float trips, scenic bus tours, charter air flights to vacation and resort areas, and the scheduling of hunting and fishing excursions in cooperation with outfitting and guide personnel. Ms. Eliason is the mother of three children. After completing high school, Ms. Eliason attended college for two and one-half years, emphasizing secretarial training and office management. Following this she was employed as a secretary for two years before becoming a full-time homemaker. She decided to reenter full-time employment and did so by seeking out her present position. She is well prepared for her job because she has the necessary secretarial and management skills combined with an outgoing and enthusiastic personality. She has the ability to meet the public well and to interest them in the programs she represents. Additionally, Ms. Eliason has had a variety of travel experiences and is perceptive of the vacation and recreation travel interests of people.

Laurie Archuleta Jerge received her master's degree in human performance and sport from New Mexico Highlands University in 1989 and her bachelor's degree in leisure administration in 1988. Upon graduation Laurie went on to become the program director for the Roswell Family YMCA. She is currently the recreation program analyst for the city of Roswell and is a certified leisure professional. She is better known as the "Voice of Roswell Recreation," as she educates and informs the public on the benefits of recreation. In her position she analyzes and assists in the development and the promotion of community recreation activities for Roswell. Laurie hosts a television program entitled "Leisure Living" that is produced by N.M.M.I. Television Productions. She regularly provides information and public service announcements to the Roswell Daily Record and is scheduled frequently on four local radio stations, where she promotes the parks and recreation movement in the Roswell community. Laurie is heard daily on local radio with the Roswell Recreation Report. She believes that the media's support has allowed her to bring to the fore the importance of the role of leisure education, and she is extremely grateful to them for the opportunity. She assists with special events and is responsible for the evaluation of programs and services. Laurie has been known to say that "To change someone's life for the better, to me, is the ultimate reward; the purpose behind the determination."

A PEOPLE-ORIENTED PROFESSION

Jobs in leisure time professions are almost exclusively people-oriented. Leisure time is a commodity possessed by people—the use of it involves people, and therefore the leadership necessary to use it effectively involves working directly with people. If you are not sincerely interested in others and do not enjoy working with them, recreation is probably not a good occupational field for you. There are, however, a few exceptions to this rule because a small percentage of the jobs are fairly isolated from direct contact with people. These would include certain jobs in natural resource management.

BE SURE OF YOUR DIRECTION

Before entering this profession or any other profession, you ought to be very analytical about the kind of work you would actually be doing and whether you would be able to achieve your professional aspirations. Additionally, you ought to be realistic about the goals you set and how you can go about reaching them. Finally, in addition to earning a living at a satisfactory level, you should want to devote your life to an occupation that is meaning-ful! The field of recreation and leisure offers you an opportunity to contribute significantly to society, and you should approach this by making your goals and aspirations achievable and then setting on a course to reach your professional potential.

CHAPTER 8

ORGANIZATIONS BENEFICIAL TO YOUR CAREER

Experience is a key component to getting a position in the leisure field. Membership and participation in professional and service organizations related to the field is a proven method for obtaining experience.

There are many professional organizations associated with recreation and parks at the state, regional, and national levels. Every state has a state association for health, physical education, and recreation as well as a recreation and park association or society. There also are district and national organizations that correspond to these. Further, there are state, district, and national organizations that relate only to specific phases of recreation and parks, such as camping, skiing, and boating. In this section it is feasible to discuss briefly only a few of the more prominent national organizations.

THE AMERICAN ALLIANCE FOR HEALTH, PHYSICAL EDUCATION, RECREATION, AND DANCE

The AAHPERD is a voluntary education organization made up of seven national associations and six district associations with fifty-four state and territorial affiliates. The membership, which exceeds fifty-five thousand, is composed of health and physical educators, coaches and athletic directors, and personnel in safety, recreation and leisure services, and dance. The organization was founded in 1885 by a group of forty-nine people, mostly educators and physicians interested in promoting "physical training." Today the membership network reaches into more than 16,000 school districts, over 2,000 colleges and universities, and over 10,000 community recreation units.

Following are the national associations that belong to the alliance:

American Association for Leisure and Recreation (AALR). Promotes school, community, and national programs of leisure services and recreation education.

American School and Community Safety Association (ASCSA). Emphasizes safety in sports and other safety concerns such as injury control, highway safety, and first aid and emergency care.

Association for the Advancement of Health Education (AAHE). Works for continuing, comprehensive programs of health education. Position papers are developed on such health topics as certification, drug education, and sex education.

Association for Research, Administration and Professional Councils and Societies (ARAPCS). Coordinates the following special interest structures: aquatics, college/university administrators, city and county directors, outdoor education, facilities, equipment and supplies, international relations, measurement and evaluation, physical fitness, therapeutics, and student members.

National Association for Girls and Women in Sport (NAGWS). Serves those involved in teaching, coaching, officiating, athletic administration, athletic training, club sports, and intramurals at the elementary, secondary, and college levels.

National Association for Sport and Physical Education (NASPE). Provides leadership opportunities in physical education and sports development and competition, consultation, publications, conferences, research, and a public information program.

National Dance Association (NDA). Promotes the development of sound policies for dance in education through conferences, convention programs, special projects, publications, and cooperation with other dance and art groups.

The AAHPERD holds a national convention each year. In addition, each of the six districts holds a district convention annually, and the fifty-four state and territorial affiliates also conduct annual conventions. The alliance and its affiliates sponsor a large number of workshops, conferences, and clinics each year, all of which are pointed toward professional development of the members or the solution of particular issues pertaining to the profession. It also conducts a job placement service.

The alliance publishes four regular periodicals—*Update, Journal of Physical Education and Recreation, Health Education,* and the *Research Quarterly.* Also, more than a dozen newsletters are prepared and distributed regularly to provide information in specific areas of the associations. The alliance publishes fifty to sixty books and films each year, the titles of which are available in the AAHPERD publications catalog. The home office of the alliance is located at 1900 Association Drive, Reston, VA 22091.

AMERICAN CAMPING ASSOCIATION

The American Camping Association was established in 1910 to further the welfare of children and adults of America through camping and to extend the recreational and educational benefits of out-of-doors living. The association serves as the voice of camp leaders throughout the nation, and it is the organization that stimulates high professional standards among camp leaders and camping agencies. It sponsors national conferences for the purpose of improving camp leadership and camp programs.

The association publishes *Camping Magazine* eight times a year. It also publishes and distributes several books and pamphlets on camping and related activities. It is financed through membership dues. The home office address is Bradford Woods, Martinsville, IN 46151.

CANADIAN ASSOCIATION FOR HEALTH, PHYSICAL EDUCATION, AND RECREATION

This association is the Canadian counterpart for the United States AAHPERD. The CAHPER is a national nonprofit voluntary organization that, since its inception in 1933, has been concerned and engaged in providing and extending the benefits of physical activity to the citizens of Canada. Its particular objectives are stated as follows:

1. To acquire and disseminate knowledge pertaining to physical activity of human beings.
2. To stimulate interest and participation in physical activity by all Canadians.
3. To promote the establishment of acceptable programs of physical activity under the direction of qualified leaders.
4. To participate actively in the establishment and the improvement of standards of practice of all who are entrusted with the responsibility of leadership in the fields of physical activity.

5. To encourage relationships among professional groups concerned with human physical activity.

6. To cooperate with any and all local, provincial, national, and international organizations that are committed to the improvement of the well-being of mankind.

The CAHPER issues a monthly periodical and a quarterly research bulletin, and it publishes numerous pamphlets and booklets on various topics of the profession. The national office is at 333 River Road, Vanier (Ottawa), Ontario, K1L 8B9.

NATIONAL EMPLOYEE SERVICES AND RECREATION ASSOCIATION

This association was formerly known as the National Industrial Recreation Association (NIRA). The NESRA is a nonprofit organization dedicated to the principle that employee recreation, fitness, and other service programs are essential to effective personnel management. The members of the association are the suppliers and directors of such programs in business, industry, and the government. The NESRA originated in 1941 and today serves more than twenty-five thousand member companies in the United States and Canada. Its official publication is *Employee Services Management,* which reaches five thousand industries ten times a year. Further, the association holds annual conferences at the national and regional levels for the purpose of disseminating useful information and updating its members on current trends and new program ideas.

NESRA promotes employee programs as a means of improving productivity and fostering good relations among the employees and between employees and management. It assists member organizations in developing, promoting, and improving recreation and other nonnegotiated employee benefits.

In addition to its monthly magazine and annual conferences, it distributes newsletters, provides product and service discounts for employee groups, disseminates program ideas, and provides consultation. It conducts five national tournaments each year. For more information, contact NESRA, 20 N. Wacker, Suite 2020, Chicago, IL 60606.

NATIONAL RECREATION AND PARK ASSOCIATION

The National Recreation and Park Association is an independent nonprofit service organization dedicated to the conservation of natural resources, the beautification of the environment, and the development, expansion, and improvement of park and recreation leadership, programs, facilities, and services for human growth and community betterment. NRPA is the only independent national organization servicing all aspects of the nation's park and recreation movement. Much of its income is raised through membership dues.

NRPA was formed in 1966 by the merger of five pioneer organizations in the park and recreation field: the American Association of Zoological Parks and Aquariums, the American Institute of Park Executives, the American Recreation Society, the National Conference on State Parks, and the National Recreation Association. It has a professional staff located at the headquarters office. Additional professional personnel in five regional offices across the United States provide in-person consultant services to park and recreation agencies and related organizations at the municipal, county, district, and state levels.

To serve each member's special interests, NRPA has seven branches: the Armed Forces Recreation Society, the American

Park and Recreation Society, the Citizen—Board Member Branch, the National Society for Park Resources, the Student Recreation and Park Society, the National Therapeutic Recreation Society, and the Society of Park and Recreation Educators.

NRPA services are generally classified into five primary categories although some overlap the others: (1) public affairs, (2) research, (3) professional services, (4) membership, and (5) executive. It also provides a job placement service.

The association sponsors numerous annual educational and planning conferences and workshops on national and regional levels. It prepares and distributes numerous books and pamphlets on park and recreation topics. The association also produces the following periodic publications:

1. *Parks and Recreation Magazine* (monthly)—designed to acquaint the general public with various park and recreation problems, trends, ideas, and policies.
2. *Management Aids*—"how to" manuals dealing with specific policy and management functions.
3. *Publications Catalog*—an annotated list of recreation books available for purchase through NRPA's Book Center.
4. *Newsletters*—a regular series of monthly, bimonthly, and quarterly news digests on topics of specific interest to professionals and lay board members in the park and recreation field.
5. *Washington Action Report*—biweekly public affairs newsletter on subscription basis.
6. *Park Practice Program*—a series of three park-related idea publications for national, regional, state, and local park administrators.
7. *Journal of Leisure Research*—a quarterly publication highlighting the most recent and pertinent research efforts in parks and recreation.

8. *TRJ (Therapeutic Recreation Journal)*—a quarterly containing articles of interest to members of the National Therapeutic Recreation Society.
9. *Dateline*—monthly newsletter to all members. The home office of the NRPA is located at 3101 Park Center Drive, Alexandria, VA 22209.

Following are other national professional or service organizations that are closely aligned with recreation and parks:

Amateur Athletic Union of the United States, Inc.
3400 W. Eighty-sixth Street
Indianapolis, IN 46268

Amateur Hockey Assn. of the U.S.
2997 Broadmoor Valley Road
Colorado Springs, CO 80906

Amateur Softball Assn. of America
2801 N.E. Fiftieth Street
Oklahoma City, OK 73111

Amateur Trapshooting Assn. of America
601 W. National Road
Vandalia, OH 45377

American Alliance for Health, Physical Education, Recreation, and
    Dance (AAHPERD)
1900 Association Drive
Reston, VA 22091–1599

American Alpine Club
113 E. Ninetieth Street
New York, NY 10028

American Assn. of Botanical Gardens and Arboreta, Inc.
P.O. Box 206
Swarthmore, PA 19081

American Assn. for Leisure and Recreation
1900 Association Drive
Reston, VA 22091

American Assn. of Museums
1225 I Street, NW
Washington, DC 20005

American Assn. of Zoological Parks and Aquariums
Oglebay Park
Wheeling, WV 26003

American Badminton Assn., Inc.
501 W. Sixth Street
Papillion, NE 68046

American Bowling Congress
5301 S. Seventy-sixth Street
Greendale, WI 53129

American Camping Assn.
5000 State Road, 67 N.
Martinsville, IN 46151

American Casting Assn.
1739 Praise Boulevard
Fenton, MO 63026

American Federation of Arts
41 E. Sixty-fifth Street
New York, NY 10021

American Folklore Society
Ohio Arts Council
727 E. Main Street
Columbus, OH 43205

American Forest Council
1250 Connecticut NW
Washington, DC 20036

American Forestry Assn.
1516 P Street, NW
Washington, DC 20005

American Horse Shows Assn.
220 E. Forty-second Street
New York, NY 10017

American Hotel and Motel Assn. (National)
1201 New York Avenue NW
Washington, DC 20005–3931

American Lawn Bowls Assn.
11660 S.W. King George
King City, OR 97224

American Motorcycle Assn.
33 Collegeview Road
Westerville, OH 43801

American Platform Tennis Assn.
Box 901
Upper Montclair, NJ 07043

American Society of Landscape Architects
1733 Connecticut NW
Washington, DC 20009

American Running and Fitness Assn.
  2001 S Street NW
  Washington, DC 20001

American Therapeutic Recreation Assn. (ATRA)
  P.O. Box 15215
  Hattiesburg, MS 39404-5215

American Water Ski Assn.
  P.O. Box 191
  799 Overlook Drive
  Winter Haven, FL 33882

American Youth Hostels, Inc.
  P.O. Box 37613
  Washington, DC 20013

Amusement Parks and Attractions International Assn.
  7222 W. Carnal Drive
  North Riverside, FL 30546

Antique Automobile Club of America, Inc.
  501 W. Governor Road
  Hershey, PA 17033

Assn. for Experiential Education (AEE)
  CU Box 249
  Boulder, CO 80309

Assn. of Interpretive Naturalists, Inc.
  P.O. Box 1892
  Fort Collins, CO 80522

Athletic Institute
  200 Castlewood
  North Palm Beach, FL 33408

Babe Ruth Baseball, Inc.
1770 Brunswick Avenue
P.O. Box 5000
Trenton, NJ 08638

Botanical Society of America, Inc.
Ecology and Evolutionary Biology
75 N. Eagleville Road
U-43 University of Connecticut
Storrs, CT 06268

Boy Scouts of America
1325 Walnut Hill Lane
P.O. Box 152079
Irving, TX 75015

Pony Baseball
P.O. Box 225
Washington, PA 15301

Camp Fire, Inc.
4601 Madison Avenue
Kansas City, MO 64112

Club Mgmt. Assn. of America
7615 Winterberry Place
P.O. Box 34482
Bethesda, MD 20817

Club Managers Assn. of America
1733 King Street
Alexandria, VA 22314–2720

Conservation Education Assn.
Oklahoma Conservation Commission
2800 Lincoln
Oklahoma City, OK 73105

Conservation Foundation
   1250 Twenty-fourth Street NW
   Washington, DC 20037

Garden Club of America
   598 Madison Avenue
   New York, NY 10022

Girl Scouts of the United States of America
   830 Third Avenue
   New York, NY 10022

Girls Clubs of America, Inc.
   30 E. Thirty-third Street
   New York, NY 10016

Hobby Industry Assn. of America, Inc.
   319 E. Fifty-fourth Street
   Elmwood Park, NJ 07407

Hotel Sales and Marketing Assn.
   1400 K Street NW
   Suite 810
   Washington, DC 20005

Ice Skating Institute of America
   1000 Skokie Boulevard
   Wilmette, IL 60091

International Assn. of Amusement Parks and Attractions
   4230 King Street
   Alexandria, VA 22302

International Assn. of Convention and Visitor Bureaus
  702 Bloomington Road
  Champaign, IL 61820

International Bicycle Touring Society
  P.O. Box 6979
  San Diego, CA 92106

International Festivals Assn. (IFA)
  P.O. Box 2950
  Port Angeles, WA 98362

International Recreation Assn.
  345 E. Forty-sixth Street
  New York, NY 10004

International Softball Congress, Inc.
  2523 W. Fourteenth Street Road
  Greeley, CO 80631

International Spin Fishing Assn.
  P.O. Box 81
  Downey, CA 90241

Izaak Walton League of America
  P.O. Box 824
  Iowa City, IA 52244

League of American Wheelmen, Inc.
  6707 Whitestone Road
  Baltimore, MD 21207

Little League Baseball
  P.O. Box 3485
  Williamsport, PA 17701

Meeting Planners International
  3719 Roosevelt Road
  Middletown, OH 45042

Men's Garden Clubs of America
  5560 Merle Hay Road
  P.O. Box 241
  Des Moines, IA 50131

National Amateur Baseball Federation
  12406 Keynote Lane
  Bowie, MD 20715

National Archery Assn. of the U.S.
  1750 E. Boulder Street
  Colorado Springs, CO 80909

National Assn. of County Park and Recreation Officials
  c/o National Assn. of Counties
  440 First Street NW
  Washington, DC 20001

National Assn. of Intercollegiate Athletics
  1221 Baltimore Street
  Kansas City, MO 64105

National Assn. of Professional Forestry Schools and Colleges
  P.O. Box 8001
  Raleigh, NC 27695

National Audubon Society
  950 Third Avenue
  New York, NY 10022

National Baseball Congress
  Box 1420
  Wichita, KA 67201

National Campers and Hikers Assn., Inc.
  7172 Transit Road
  Buffalo, NY 14043

National Camping Association
  Bradford Woods
  Martinsville, IN 46151

National Certified Therapeutic Recreation Council (NCTRC)
  49 S. Main, Suite 005
  Spring Valley, NY 10977

National Collegiate Athletic Assn.
  P.O. Box 1906
  Nall Avenue at Sixty-third Street
  Mission, KS 66201

The National Community Education Assn.
  1030 Fifteenth Street
  Washington, DC 20005

National Council of State Garden Clubs, Inc.
  4401 Magnolia Avenue
  St. Louis, MO 63110

National Duckpin Bowling Congress
  4609 Horizon Circle
  Baltimore, MD 21208

National Employee Services and Recreation Assn. (NESRA)
  2211 York Road
  Oak Brook, IL 60521

National Field Archery Assn.
  31407 Outer I-10
  Redlands, CA 92373

National Golf Foundation, Inc.
  Rte. 3, Box 210
  Hwy. 89, N.
  Flagstaff, AZ 86004

National Industrial Recreation Association
  2400 S. Downing
  Westchester, IL 60154

National Institute on Parks and Grounds Mgmt.
  P.O. Box 1936
  Appleton, WI 54913

National Intramural Recreation and Sports Assn. (NIRSA)
  Dixon Recreation Center
  Oregon State University
  Corvallis, OR 97331

National Junior College Athletic Association
  P.O. Box 7305
  Colorado Springs, CO 80933

National Marine Manufacturers Assn.
  410 N. Michigan Avenue
  Chicago, IL 60611

National Model Railroad Assn. Inc.
  4121 Cromwell Road
  Chattanooga, TN 37421

National Parks and Conservation Association
   1015 Thirty-first Street NW
   Washington, DC 20007

National Public Park Tennis Assn.
   3325 Wilshire Boulevard
   Los Angeles, CA 90010

National Recreation and Parks Assn.
   2775 South Quincy Street
   Suite 300
   Arlington, VA 22206–2204

National Rifle Association
   1600 Rhode Island Avenue NW
   Washington, DC 20036

National Shuffleboard Assn., Inc.
   c/o Grove Trailer Estates
   P.O. Box 5441
   Bradenton, FL 34281

National Skeet Shooting Assn.
   P.O. Box 680007
   San Antonio, TX 78268

National Ski Areas Assn.
   P.O. Box 48085
   Denver, CO 80248

National Spa and Pool Institute
   2111 Eisenhower Avenue
   Alexandria, VA 22314

National Therapeutic Recreation Society
   3101 Park Center Drive
   Alexandria, VA 22302

National Trust for Historic Preservation
   1785 Massachusetts Avenue NW
   Washington, DC 20036

National Wildlife Federation
   1400 Sixteenth Street NW
   Washington, DC 20036

North American Yacht Racing Union
   37 W. Forty-fourth Street
   New York, NY 10036

Photographic Society of America
   3000 Union Founders Boulevard
   Oklahoma City, OK 73112

Pop Warner Jr. League Football
   1041 Western Savings Bank Building
   Philadelphia, PA 19107

Recreation Industrial Assn.
   P.O. Box 204
   Chantilly, VA 22021

Recreation Vehicle Industry Assn.
   P.O. Box 204
   Chantilly, VA 22021

Resort and Commercial Recreation Assn. (RCRA)
P.O. Box 1208
New Port Richey, FL 34656

Rodeo Cowboys Association
2529 W. Nineteenth Avenue
Denver, CO 80204

The Roundtable Associates, Inc. (RTA)
404 Highgate Terrace
Silver Springs, MD 20904

Sierra Club
730 Polk Street
San Francisco, CA 94109

Society of American Foresters
5400 Grosvenor Lane
Bethesda, MD 20814

Sporting Goods Manufacturing Assn. (SGMA)
200 Castlewood Drive
North Palm Beach, FL 33480

Travel Industry Association of America
2 Lafayette Center
1133 Twenty-first Street NW
Washington, DC 20036

U.S. Chess Federation
479 Broadway
Newburgh, NY 12550

U.S. Fencing Association
1750 Boulder Street
Colorado Springs, CO 80909

U.S. Field Hockey Assn.
1750 E. Boulder Street
Colorado Springs, CO 80909

U.S. Figure Skating Assn.
20 First Street
Colorado Springs, CO 80906

U.S. Golf Association
P.O. Box 708
Far Hills, NJ 07931

U.S. Gymnastics Federation
201 S. Capitol
Indianapolis, IN 46225

U.S. Handball Association
930 N. Benton Avenue
Tucson, AZ 85711

U.S. Judo Federation
967 Maybury Avenue
Santa Fe, CA 95133

U.S. Parachute Association
1440 Duke Street
Alexandria, VA 22314

U.S. Polo Association
4059 Iron Works Pike
Lexington, KY 40511

U.S. Squash Racquets Assn.
211 Ford Road
Bala Cynwyd, PA 19004

U.S. Table Tennis Association
  1750 E. Boulder Street
  Colorado Springs, CO 80909

U.S. Tennis Assn., Inc.
  1212 Avenue of the Americas
  New York, NY 10036

U.S. Volleyball Association
  1750 E. Boulder Street
  Colorado Springs, CO 80909

Wilderness Education Assn.
  20 Winona Avenue, Box 89
  Saranac Lake, NY 12983

Wilderness Society
  1400 I Street NW
  Washington, DC 20005

Wildlife Management Institute
  111 Fourteenth Street NW
  Washington, DC 20005

Wildlife Society
  5410 Grosvenor Lane
  Bethesda, MD 20814

World Tourism Organization
  Avenida del Generalissimo 59
  Madrid 16
  Spain

Young Men's Christian Assn. of the United States of America
    National Council
    101 N. Wacker Drive
    Chicago, IL 60606

Young Women's Christian Assn. of the United States of America
    726 Broadway
    New York, NY 10003

CHAPTER 9

KEEPING UP WITH THE TIMES

Americans spend about a third of their income on leisure pursuits. In the 1990s consumers spent approximately $280 billion on recreational goods and services, constituting about 7 percent of all consumer spending. This figure is expected to continue to rise. Leisure is expected to be the number one industry by the new millennium.

In light of the fact that recreation and leisure time job opportunities are becoming prominent, it is especially important that prospective members of the occupational field be well informed about recent changes and present trends, including both the positive and negative aspects. Following are explanations of some of the more important changes and trends.

GOVERNMENT RESTRAINTS

Local government recreation and park agencies have constituted the main stream of employment in the area of recreation and park management. Further, the number of such agencies and their ability to employ recreation leaders has increased tremendously since World War II, with the fastest rate of increase occurring during the 1960s and early 1970s. This increase has been the main contributing factor to the tremendous expansion of recreation and park major programs in colleges and universities. It is a fact, however, that during the 1980s municipal recreation and park programs remained at a fairly constant level, meaning there was very little increase in job opportunities in these programs during that decade.

Also, leisure time employment in federal and state agencies remained at near the same level during the decade of the 1980s. This is because of public pressure for reduced government spending and nonexpansion of government services.

TRAVEL

It appears that the increased cost of travel is here to stay, and this is having a curtailing effect on the amount of travel that people do for all purposes, including travel for pleasure. Consequently, jobs that relate to the tourist industry have increased at a slower rate than earlier predictions. The rate of gradual increase will likely continue during the foreseeable future, and this will have particular effect on resort areas and recreation places far away from the population.

FOUR-DAY WORKWEEK

There has been a considerable amount of experimentation in American industry with the four-day workweek. In most cases the four-day workweek consists of ten-hour days, so that the total for the week is still forty hours. But some companies have gone to a thirty-six-hour week made up of four nine-hour days. The American Management Association reported that of the companies it surveyed, 6 percent were involved with the four-day workweek either for all or part of its employees. Another 18 percent were studying the four-day workweek but had not yet decided to implement it. One percent had experimented with it and then discarded the idea. This means that approximately 25 percent of the companies surveyed by the AMA were either involved with a four-day workweek or were considering adopting it.

POPULATION SHIFTS

Currently slightly more than three-fourths of the people in America live in urban and suburban areas. By the year 2000, 78 percent of the 280 million people will live in these areas. By then the eastern seaboard, Great Lakes area, the West Coast, and the southern gulf region will each represent a sprawling megapolis. Also, the Rocky Mountains region and the Sunbelt area of the Southwest will be much more populated than they are now.

Recently there has been an indication of a shift from suburbs to cities in the middle-class and upper-class residential areas. Undoubtedly this has been encouraged by traffic congestion and the increased costs of commuting, and the trend is having a stimulating effect on the rehabilitation of urban areas.

Another noticeable shift of population is from the industrial areas of the East and Midwest to the Sunbelt regions of the South and Southwest. This is partly influenced by employment opportunities and partly by the migration of retirees which, in turn, helps to stimulate employment opportunities in the Sunbelt region.

TECHNOLOGICAL ADVANCES

During recent decades we have had great advances in technology, and these advances have influenced practically every aspect of our lives including what we do for recreation, where we do it, and how much time we spend doing it. In the future, technology will have even greater effects on recreation patterns. New devices used for participation will continue to develop and the further advancement of technology will open new worlds of leisure time activities. Technology will be both a friend and an enemy to recreation because while it will enhance recreation participation, it also will be destructive to certain portions of the recreation environment. Air pollution, water pollution, land pollution, and acid rain result partly from the industrialized aspect of modern technology.

RESOURCE SUPPLY

The supply of basic resources (namely land and water) for recreation will not increase. Certain modifications and improvements can enhance the usefulness of some of the resources, but such revisions have limited potential. On the other hand, there seems to be no limit to the potential increase in demands on the resources, and it is well established that the demands will escalate at an ever increasing rate. This simple relationship between supply and demand means that in the future we will need to: (1) more thoroughly identify the areas of high recreation potential and prevent the needed resources from being committed on a permanent basis to less essential uses; (2) continue at an increased rate to alter and improve certain resources so that they will better serve the increased demands; and (3) modify our participation in recreation activities to a level that can be accommodated by the available resources.

FUTURE PARTICIPATION TRENDS

During recent years the overall participation in recreation activities has increased about 50 percent faster than the population. This has been due to several influencing factors that have already been discussed in Chapter 3, primarily increased leisure time, increased means, and a more favorable philosophy toward participation in recreational activities.

Naturally, there will be changes in the popularity of different recreation activities and some new forms of participation will become possible due to technology. For the most part the changes will be moderate and the emphasis will continue to be on the simple and traditional forms of recreation such as hiking, cycling, camping, fishing, hunting, swimming, cultural events, and athletic participation. However, there will be a continued increase in high risk activities (river running, skydiving, hang gliding, rock climbing); winter sports, especially cross-country and downhill skiing and snowmobiling; water sports, particularly wind surfing, waterskiing, and underwater exploration; health-related activities with emphasis upon physical fitness; and wilderness experiences.

Beaches and waterways are particularly attractive for recreation, and the population tends to cluster along these areas for reasons of both commerce and recreation. Because of this, proper use and management of beaches and water corridors will be of crucial importance in the future. It is also true that places of great beauty and unique natural features will continue to grow in popularity at a disproportionate rate. Unfortunately, many of these have fragile features that must be protected from abuse and overuse.

With people's increased awareness about the need to maintain an acceptable level of physical fitness and health, leisure time will become increasingly occupied by activities that promote fitness. There will be more joggers, more cyclists, more golfers, more tennis players, and more participants in practically every popular form of fitness activity. Hopefully, there will also be more emphasis on other aspects of the healthy life such as weight control and discretion in the use of tobacco, alcohol, drugs, and other harmful substances.

There is recognition of the need to broaden the recreation program content in the area of the cultural arts and to utilize more fully the personnel in organizations within the community to expand and improve cultural arts opportunities. The emphasis on creativity as a desirable use of leisure time will have an increasing positive effect on more extensive participation and cultural activities.

Recently there has been an upsurge in private campgrounds, luxury marinas, tennis complexes, resort villages, hunting and fishing preserves, and amusement complexes such as Disneyworld and Marineland. Future technology will contribute to continued change with the prospects of plastic snow and ice for skiing and skating, double and triple deck golf driving ranges, artificial surfs for swimming and surfing, artificial white-water courses, programmed travel packages, underwater exploration vehicles, and a multitude of other leisure time innovations. We can only speculate about how rapidly these and other innovations will take hold and what changes they will cause in leisure time patterns. But it is important for us to be insightful and predictive about such matters.

All told, the most useful and most used recreation areas and facilities will be those close to the population—places that can be reached conveniently on a daily and weekend basis without excessive travel and expense. The majority of the population will concentrate on recreational opportunities that are convenient and close at hand.

BETTER LEADERSHIP

It is generally agreed that there is no substitute for adequate leadership. Regardless of what else is done by way of support, the results of an organization or a program will not exceed the level of its leadership.

Leadership preparation in the leisure sciences must enable individuals to deal successfully with rapidly changing leisure options. Within one future life span recreation seems destined to be more varied and dynamic than at any equal time in the past. Young professionals who are now entering the field will likely be engaged beyond the year 2020. It is obviously important to develop young leaders who are versatile and who will furnish adequate leadership over a long period under rapidly changing circumstances. It seems certain that our world thirty years in the future will be even more unlike the world of today than today is different from the world of thirty years ago.

On the surface it appears that professional leadership preparation is the responsibility of colleges and universities, but this is only partially true because the growth and development of professionals must be continuous. This comes about with valuable on-the-job experience, some of which must be in the form of in-service training such as conferences, institutes, and clinics; regular reading of professional literature; and tutoring from those who are professionally more mature and better informed.

The leadership in recreation will need to come from a combination of well-prepared resource management specialists (to plan and manage parks and natural resources), recreation programming specialists, and a multitude of others who are specialized in such areas as landscape architecture, horticulture, wildlife, cultural arts, sports education, travel, and numerous other interests that contribute to the recreational fulfillment of the population.

Some of the most important leaders in the future will be connoisseurs who have broad perspectives and keen insights into cultural change and individual tastes and preferences. Such leaders will have to demonstrate an accurate feel for the interests of people and for the wise use of resources for both the immediate and long-term future.

OTHER TRENDS AND CHANGES

Education for the worthy use of leisure will become an evermore important responsibility of schools and other educational agencies. Creative and ingenious leadership will be required in connection with program and class content.

There will be a strong trend toward increased use of schools and other public facilities for recreational activities when the facilities are not in use for their primary purposes.

We will see significant increases in employment for recreation therapists, recreationists in corrective institutions, private club employees such as golf, tennis, and swimming instructors; managers and programmers at resorts, recreation directors for large condominium complexes and retirement villages; leaders of industrial recreation programs; and program leaders for special populations (senior citizens, single adult, handicapped).

The market for services, supplies, and equipment used in leisure activities will boom, and this will result in considerable expansion of job opportunities in leisure-related manufacturing and business.

Jobs with such voluntary youth agencies as the Boy Scouts, YMCA and YWCA, and boys and girls clubs will continue to increase as in the recent past.

There will be an accelerated trend toward creativity in the design of playgrounds, play equipment, and recreational centers.

Standard equipment and facility designs that have been with us for a long time will become obsolete.

Professional qualifications of job candidates will increase as fast as the supply of qualified personnel will permit. There will be a steady trend for job applicants to have better credentials. In response to this, professional preparation programs will become more stringent. In turn, this will cause college major programs to become more standardized, and they will be subjected to accreditation by regional and national accrediting agencies.

One of the adjustments that is taking place and will continue in the future is a more even spread of facility use during the week as compared to weekends. This is due to a combination of factors including: (1) the increased percentage of the population who is of the retired or partially retired status and whose time availability is the same on Tuesday as on Saturday; (2) later entry by youth into the job market and more availability of discretionary time by youth; (3) the trend toward more involvement with the four-day work-week; and (4) the continued reduction in the average workweek (it is now about thirty-six hours for the majority of the nation's "full-time" employees).

With the attitude toward more stringent controls on government spending and with projected continued financial affluency, there will be a marked increase in commercialized recreation. Those with good business minds will find many opportunities to capitalize on people's leisure time interests in terms of financial profit. Hopefully, the commercializers will demonstrate sound judgment about what is good for society and keep exploitation to a minimum. The recreation professionals will have to guard against such imbalances along the way. This can be done by bringing community pressure against undesirable commercialism and by sponsoring appealing programs through community agencies that will combat the popularizing of undesirable commercial activities.

LEISURE COUNSELING

It appears that sometime in the foreseeable future leisure counseling will become a branch of the profession. The counseling will be primarily in the form of helping people review the leisure time segment of their lives and which alternatives are open to them in view of each one's particular skills, interests, and financial status. The counselor will help people crystallize their thinking about what they would like to do and what they want to become in terms of leisure time participants, and how they can go about achieving their objectives. Another aspect will be the counseling of people who have particular physical, social, and psychological problems of a kind that leisure time activities can help solve.

An accelerated research effort will be needed to accumulate the information that will be necessary to give appropriate direction to the various facets of the leisure time movement. Much of the research will take place on college and university campuses. But some of it will be conducted through nonschool agencies.

STRETCHING THE MIND

In two or three decades from now, another author will be able to write about changes that are equally as dramatic as the changes we are experiencing. He or she may talk about sightseeing tours in outer space or excursions deep under the sea in capsules or glass submarines. That author may lament the plight of the wilderness hiker before the development of individualized flying devices that silently carry recreationists to mountain tops and once remote fishing, hunting, and scenic areas. That writer may refer to new forms of computerized golf and baseball designed especially for less space. He or she will probably speak of the more affluent individuals who have personal counselors to help select and arrange leisure time pursuits and may even mention reservations made for those persons on Moon Flight 732.

These ideas may seem far-fetched, but not many years ago it would have been just as far-fetched to talk seriously about making twenty-five ski runs from the top of Beaver Mountain in one day, or taking a weekend hunting trip to Alaska, or waterskiing behind a power boat traveling at 30 m.p.h.

It is possible that these futuristic projections are not really far-fetched or, in fact, even far away.

.

APPENDIX A

FEDERAL AND STATE AGENCIES

The following federal agencies have major responsibilities in recreation and therefore hire recreation personnel. A number of other federal agencies are involved in recreation less extensively and less directly.

Department of Agriculture
Washington, DC 20250
    Extension Services
    Forest Service
    Soil Conservation Service

Department of Defense
Washington, DC 20301
    The several branches of the
    military
    U.S. Army Corps of
    Engineers

Department of Health, Education,
    and Welfare
Washington, DC 20201
    U.S. Office of Education
    Office of Environmental
    Education

Department of Housing and Urban
    Development
Washington, DC 20410

Department of the Interior
Washington, DC 20240
    Bureau of Sports, Fisheries,
    and Wildlife
    National Park Service
    Bureau of Land Management
    Bureau of Reclamation

Department of Transportation
Washington, DC 20990

Even though each state is organized differently, all states have offices that formulate and oversee recreation policy. Following are the divisions of state government that typically have recreation and park responsibilities:

Department of State Parks
Department of Wildlife
Department of Forests
Travel and Tourism Division
Water Resources Division

POTENTIAL EMPLOYING ORGANIZATIONS

Because of the diversified nature of leisure activities and leisure occupations, it is not feasible to list all of the employing organizations. But the following list will be helpful:

Federal government recreation and park related agencies (see Appendix A)

State government recreation and park related agencies (see Appendix A)

Municipal, county, and district recreation and park departments

Community education programs

Commercial recreation enterprises, such as dude ranches, ski areas, and summer resorts

Private clubs for golf, tennis, and swimming

Recreation and park departments in colleges and universities

Hospitals and nursing homes with recreation therapy programs

Industrial organizations that sponsor employee recreation

Correctional institutions

Professional and service organizations (see Chapter 8)

Large youth-serving organizations such as the Boy Scouts, Girl Scouts, Boys Clubs, and Girls Clubs